I've travelled the world twice over,
Met the famous: saints and sinners,
Poets and artists, kings and queens,
Old stars and hopeful beginners,
I've been where no-one's been before,
Learned secrets from writers and cooks
All with one library ticket
To the wonderful world of books.

© Janice James.

The wisdom of the ages
Is there for you and me,
The wisdom of the ages,
In your local library.

There's large print books
And talking books,
For those who cannot see,
The wisdom of the ages,
It's fantastic, and it's free.

Written by Sam Wood, aged 92

THE BRONTË SISTERS' SEARCH FOR LOVE

Dilys Gater sets out to show that the Brontës' behaviour and their books resulted from their deprivation of love. The loss of their mother and two elder sisters, combined with the absence of any affection from Mr Brontë, turned them into emotional cripples who were yet able to transform their unhappiness into great literature. Why did the heroines of the Brontë novels crave so painfully for love? There are innumerable books on the Brontës, but THE BRONTË SISTERS' SEARCH FOR LOVE does have something new to say.

DILYS GATER

THE BRONTË SISTERS' SEARCH FOR LOVE

Complete and Unabridged

ULVERSCROFT
Leicester

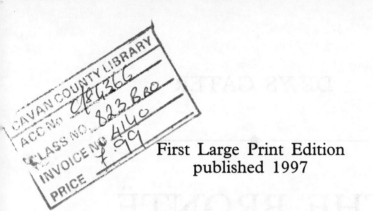

First Large Print Edition
published 1997

British Library CIP Data

Gater, Dilys
    The Brontë sisters' search for love.
    —Large print ed.—
    Ulverscroft large print series: non-fiction
    1. Brontë, Charlotte, *1816 – 1855*—Relations with men
    2. Brontë, Emily, *1818 – 1848*—Relations with men
    3. Brontë, Anne, *1820 – 1849*—Relations with men
    4. Large type books
    I. Title
    823.8′09

    ISBN 0–7089–3773–X

Published by
F. A. Thorpe (Publishing) Ltd.
Anstey, Leicestershire

Set by Words & Graphics Ltd.
Anstey, Leicestershire
Printed and bound in Great Britain by
T. J. International Ltd., Padstow, Cornwall

This book is printed on acid-free paper

Because I was so much luckier
than the Brontës

this book is for

Rizead the magician, spinner of
rainbows, spells and stars

I could not sleep: through that wild
    siege
My heart had fiercely burned and
    bounded;
The outward tumult seemed to assuage
The inward tempest it surrounded.

Emily Brontë

Contents

Preface

This book sets out to show that the Brontës' behaviour and their books resulted from their deprivation of love. The loss of their mother and two elder sisters, combined with the absence of any affection from Mr Brontë, turned the Brontës into emotional cripples who were yet able to transform their unhappiness into great literature. The book is eminently readable and even persuasive.

Why did the heroines of the Brontë novels crave so painfully for love, and why were the heroines so poorly endowed with fathers? We feel that Dilys Gater's theories may be right, both about Mr Brontë and also Maria Brontë, whose abnormal goodness is seen as part of the pattern of deprivation. By the time we get on to the three famous Brontë sisters we feel that she has stated her case.

There are innumerable books on the

Brontës, but THE BRONTË SISTERS'
SEARCH FOR LOVE does have something
new to say.

Dr Tom Winnifrith
University of Warwick.

Author's Note

What is the fascination of the Brontë sisters, those thin, nervy girls who still haunt the bleak moorland round their Yorkshire home, now a museum to perpetuate their memory? Why is Haworth Parsonage one of the most visited literary shrines in England, surpassed only by the birthplace of Shakespeare?

The spell weaved by the Brontës is that we can view them as a whole world in microcosm. Their lives were very restricted, but almost every type of human experience can be found when we examine their stories. From the triumphant achievement of genius to the bitter tragedy of abuse, abandonment and early death, every effort a human being can make and every small pleasure friendship and family love can bring are represented here. Passion, unrequited love, spiritual fulfilment, illness physical and mental, delusions, humble acceptance of achievement, ordinary living as human beings — we can find all of these in the lives of the Brontës. Everyone can find something about them to identify with and to feel a personal empathy. They belong to literature — but first, they were human beings and as such they belong to the world.

Part One

The Legacy of the Past

Introduction

IF the Brontës were to pay a visit to a modern psychiatrist, they would give him enough material for many books, not just one. Out of the six children Maria Branwell bore to her husband Patrick Brontë, there was only one possible example — their second daughter, Elizabeth — of a personality which was able to develop in anything like a reasonable manner, and even Elizabeth's case is debatable, since there are so few details available about her so that no satisfactory conclusion can be drawn. The other children, even Maria who was to die before she reached her thirteenth birthday, displayed symptoms of severe personality disorder which was of course never recognised as such and was consequently never treated in any way whatsover, no treatment being available at the time even if the Brontë pride had unbent enough for the family to admit that help may have been needed.

3

Naturally, there were may other Victorian children who suffered — cases of personality disorder and the attempts of the sufferers to try and come to terms with what seem to be the insurmountable impossibilities of living are by no means confined to this century and the psychiatrist's couch. Elizabeth I, though a great queen, is a very interesting example of a woman whose early experiences crippled her emotionally for life.

What is particularly significant about the Brontës, however, is the fact that not just one child in the family — or even two — was to experience traumas so shattering that they were never to be overcome. It was a family thing, something that arose from their own particular heredity, the events of their early years, their environment, and especially the attitude of their immediate family and those concerned with their care and welfare. In all probability, if there had been ten little Brontës instead of six, the others would have been affected to a similar degree.

At an early age, the children lost their mother, and this loss was further compounded by the death of their eldest sister Maria, who had taken on the "Little Mother" role, and whom they dearly loved. The circumstances of Maria's death, as is widely known, affected Charlotte in particular so deeply that it festered in her subconscious and it was not until many years after the event that she was to use the death of "Helen Burns" at "Lowood School" as a partial catharsis. This loss of their mother marked the beginning of what was to continue as a pattern of extreme deprivation for all the children.

In later years, when she was shown her mother's letters by her father, Charlotte recorded her feelings of desolation and loss.

"The papers were yellow with time, all having been written before I was born. It was strange now to peruse for the first time the records of a mind whence mine own sprang; and most strange and to me sad and sweet, to find that mind of a truly fine, pure and elevated order. They were written for Papa before they were married. There is a rectitude, a refinement, a constancy,

5

a modesty, a sense, a gentleness about them indescribable. I wish she had lived and that I had known her."

All children need adult models they know well to assist them in the formation of their own developing personalities. Girls will naturally use their mothers, either positively or negatively, and deprived of the mother, they will turn to a mother substitute or mother figure. In the case of the little Brontë girls, there was no mother figure to whom they could attach themselves in any satisfactory manner, though two females came to play a large part in their lives. Tabitha Aykroyd, known to them as "Tabby", arrived as a servant at the Parsonage some time after the death of Mrs Brontë, and this elderly Yorkshirewoman who grew fond of them as if they were her own "childer" took on some of the qualities of a surrogate mother (though there was always a barrier between them, for it was never forgotten that Tabby was a servant and they were young ladies.)

She, however, meant infinitely more to them emotionally than did their Aunt, Elizabeth Branwell. Aunt Branwell, their mother's sister, came from Penzance to nurse the dying Mrs Brontë, and remained at Haworth until her own death, taking charge of the children and running the household. In the absence of their own mother, the girls could not help patterning themselves to some extent on their Aunt, since they had no other model, but this was to prove more harmful than beneficial, and they never established any sort of loving relationship with Miss Branwell. Undoubtedly she was fond of her nieces, but she did not give them the physical closeness they so desperately needed, nor the unquestioning acceptance and encouragement that would have helped them to flower into normal young womanhood. Aunt's influence was a repressive one against which they had to struggle to establish their own personalities.

Much of this book will be concerned with the Brontë children's lack of the physical closeness already mentioned. Such a lack is extremely harmful to a young individual, and the complete absense of any sort of physical expression of love can cripple children emotionally for life.

It would be stimulating to hear what Thomas A. Harris, the psychiatrist whose handbook to Transactional Analysis "I'm OK — You're OK" sold in the millions, would make of the Brontës, but of particular relevance here is one basic point he underlines in his book:

"Stroking, or repetitious bodily contact, is essential to (the individual's) survival. Without it he will die, if not physically, then psychologically."

Dr Harris takes this further by mentioning the condition known as marasmus, which is literally a complete absence of any form of "stroking" or emotional body contact. In the days of "foundling homes" for unwanted babies, the infants were only given the most cursory of care, fed and kept warm; they received no love, attention, cuddling or bodily contact whatsover. As a result, many of them died of marasmus. There was nothing physically wrong with them. It was as if they realised instintively that they mattered to no-one, and the thought was too much to bear, they could not live with this awful knowledge.

Even today, scientists are experimenting with the whole question of touch, and seeing what happens, for instance, when baby animals are allowed to see, but not experience contact with the parent. The results are astounding. Immense deprivation symptoms can be clearly observed. And so far as children are concerned although the "foundling homes" are mercifully no longer a part of our society, emotional troubles can often occur in long stay centres for children, where the staff are too overworked to give the inmates much cuddling or physical contact.

In the case of the Brontë girls, although the loss of their mother was to have enormous repercussions, I believe that the deepest loss they suffered — amazing though it may seem — was the lack of a father.

At first sight, such a suggestion will seem ridiculous, for not only did the girls have a father, but he in fact outlived them all and was, on the surface, one of the strongest and most powerful influence in their lives. They owed their home, their education, their position in society — everything — to their father. They lived under the same roof as he did, they were hardly ever separated, they were dutifully devoted to "Papa".

But did they love him? And did he love them?

On the surface, of course they did. Yet there are questions which need to be examined. Did they suceed in establishing a satisfactory father-daughter relationship, or did each of them go through their comparatively short lives unconsciously seeking the love and affection that they felt had been denied them by their father? Did they create father-figures in their work, in the guise of lovers? Did they feel a sense of loss, of having been robbed, that left them emotionally retarded, unable to regard men as human beings like themselves but seeing them as either as larger-than-life, or hopelessly weak and rather contemptible? Was each of them doomed never to have a happily fulfilled relationship with a man from their earliest years?

It is interesting to note that Charlotte declared that from the age of twelve, she had resigned herself to being an old maid.

It might be argued that it was the fault of the system that made Mr Brontë remote and withdrawn from his daughters. Victorian fathers were notoriously undemonstrative — in public, at any rate. But what about in private? A Victorian father could — and quite often did — indulge his affection for his little girls if he wanted to. Yet it seems that, sadly, Mr Brontë did not want to.

The first part of this book will outline the characters of each of the people who influenced the young Brontës during their early years. With a knowledge of these personalities, we can go on to consider how they, as well as circumstances and environment, shaped and moulded the children into the adults they later became — adults who, suffering from overwhelming loss and deprivation, made of their lives a desperate journey in search of love.

Patrick Brontë

THE first indisputable facts about the girls' father are that he was born in 1777 in County Down, Ireland. His own father, Hugh Brunty, was a farm labourer and a Protestant. His mother Eleanor (or Alice) McClory, was a Catholic, but on her marriage in 1776, she renounced her faith and turned Protestant like her husband. Their first child, Patrick Brunty, was born on St Patrick's Day, Monday 17th March, the following year; and their home at that time was a two-roomed thatched cabin in the wilds, though later the family moved to better accommodation.

During the first nineteen years of Patrick's life, his mother produced nine more children, so that he himself was the eldest of ten. These particular children were regarded as "heathens" by their neighbours because they were born of a mixed religious marriage, so the other local children were not permitted to associate with them. The result, one might have thought, would have been that they grew very close and fond of each other. But on examination, this does not seem to have been the case — at least as far as Patrick was concerned.

He appears to have taken little or no interest in his new brothers and sisters as they appeared on the scene, and there does not seem to be any indication that he felt any strong ties towards them. Later, when he had left Ireland and gone to England to "make his fortune", he did send money regularly to his mother, little though he could afford it, but it is doubtful whether he ever thought much about the other nine young people who made up his family circle – a strange and un-Irish characteristic.

Patrick, whose sole motives in life were to raise himself by means of his own efforts, out of the mould of farm labourer, and to educate himself, as indeed he did with much doggedness and persistence, found the constant requirements of a young family irksome. He would shut his ears to the hungry cries of each new baby as he spelt out the words he was trying to read, and more than likely, he disregarded invitations from the others to "Come and play with us" in order to be by himself to study.

In fact, he seems to have been born without any childish streak whatsoever. There are no tales told of him ever playing games, jokes, or getting into youthful scrapes. Indeed, biographers recount proudly how from his earliest years he spent all the spare time he could in painstakingly stumbling through his father's library of four books until he knew large chunks of them by heart, and wandering amongst the hills brooding on the wonders of nature.

Not that there is anything wrong in this. He was obviously a highly imaginative and quick-minded child who enjoyed mental, rather than physical, stimulation — and who was blessed with a physique that made it possible for him to indulge in "book-learning" without his peers making fun of his ambition and cleverness. He had the best of both worlds, all in all. He was intelligent to a startling degree, yet his appearance and his natural charm meant that he could be accepted by the others.

Extremely bright children are often the object of cruelty and jibes from others who are not so bright — but this never seems to have happened with Patrick.

He began to work at the age of twelve as an assistant to a blacksmith, but his ambition was ferocious. It was probably fanned by the fact that on one occasion, while he was shoeing the horse of a gentleman, he overheard the blacksmith and the man in question talking about what, exactly, was meant by that term "gentleman". The blacksmith gave it as his solemn opinion that his boy assistant was definitely "a gentleman by nature", and Patrick never forgot this incident.

Undoubtedly, he thought of himself as "a cut above" the rest of his family. Certainly he did manage to make his way in the world, a remarkable feat for a child who had been born in a two-roomed cabin, to a farm labourer and his wife. And without that inner conviction that somehow, he was better than the rest of them, he would never have made the psychological change, and probably would never have undertaken the practical physical effort necessary for him to climb the ladder in an extremely class-conscious society.

Undoubtedly, he was a snob. But his character was far more complicated than at first appears. Let us follow him a little further in his career, and we will begin to see a pattern emerging.

From blacksmith's assistant, he went to work for a weaver and became an apprentice. He worked hard, buying what books he could in his self-imposed task of educating his mind and expanding it, and spent his leisure time in reading, learning and declaiming aloud.

He changed his employer and went to a man called Clibborn, where he worked at making very fine webs — something which caused his eyesight to suffer in later years. But again, whenever he had any free time, he would be out on the hills, reading and declaiming from whatever book was to hand.

The fact that he was fond of declaiming verse aloud is an interesting one. It suggests that (had the theatre been a respectable profession) Patrick might have considered becoming an actor. Certainly he had an actor's instincts — and

16

when we bear in mind that acting is closely associated with writing, his early inclinations to declaim aloud take on a significance that will become apparent later, when we come to consider the development of his children.

It was while he was out declaiming to air and sky that he attracted the attention of the Rev. Andrew Harshaw, a Presbyterian minister who, though he had been ambitious himself had had to make do with a position as teacher at the village school at Ballynafern, and found it frustrating. Now here, thought the Reverend, as he watched and listened to the fifteen-year-old boy, here was someone who looked as if he was promising material. What might he not achieve with a good education?

He introduced himself and made his offer. From his well-stocked library, Patrick should be allowed to borrow whatever books he liked. That in itself seemed like Paradise to the lad who loved words. But there was more. If, in his long and busy working day, he could spare the hours, Harshaw promised he would personally instruct Patrick in the classics

17

and mathematics, with the objective of the boy becoming a teacher himself. It was only to be expected that Patrick accepted with alacrity, and no-one can do other than admire the whole-heartedness with which he applied himself to studying every spare moment he could, as well as carrying on with his work in the weaving trade.

Certainly it cannot be said that he did not deserve to get on, for it was a remarkable feat for a self-educated lad to grasp the fundamentals of Greek, Latin and mathematics (and later, other subjects) so that, in the following year, when he was sixteen, he was able to apply successfully (under the Rev. Harshaw's guidance and recommendation) for the post of teacher with the Glascar Hill Presbyterian Church School — and so take the first step up the social ladder that was to bring him eventually to Haworth.

We know that Patrick continued as a teacher until he was twenty-five, first at the Glascar Hill Presbyterian Church School, and later at the larger school at Drumballyroney, where he also taught

18

the Rector's sons. By all accounts, he was wise, advanced and enlightened in his methods of teaching, and far ahead of his time. This we must not deny him. But what is a teacher? Could it not be that Patrick took to the profession because (like acting) it gave him a captive audience to talk to, to declaim to, to try to instil with his own knowledge and beliefs?

Whatever his motives, he dedicated his days to teaching, even going so far as to spend his own time also with both brighter and duller pupils, taking them on excursions, and seeing their parents to discuss the progress of each child.

On the surface, it seems that here we have a really generous, self-sacrificing man. What has happened to the vain snob we saw earlier? The answer is that he was still as much of a snob as ever, but that teaching gave him a good deal of satisfaction. He needed an audience, and for the time being, he was satisfied with his audience of village children and their parents. In his position as teacher, he was "Sir", the God-like figure to whom everyone bowed. He was

19

all-powerful in the classroom, dispensing knowledge in the way he chose, interfered with by no-one, moulding the children's personalities. The sense of power must have been tremendous to a lad born in a cabin — and recognition and power was what Patrick craved.

Several other interesting facts emerge at about this period. One reinforces the theory that Patrick had delusions of grandeur. He was not content with his surname, and varied it at times from Brunty to Pruty, Prunty and Branty. On his entry into Cambridge in 1802, however, he made it clear that henceforth, he wished to be known as Patrick Brontë. It is significant that his early hero, Nelson, had in 1799 been created Duke of Brontë, and Patrick wished to follow in footsteps that he felt were worthy of him.

It might be argued that the growing young man was no more and no less than the wise and enlightened teacher he appeared, but if that had been so, surely he would have been satisfied with his teaching position at Drumballyroney? He had already wiped the mud of farm labourer, as it were, from his boots.

But no. He made up his mind that he wanted to enter the Ministry, involving further outlay of finance, and years of further study. It might be thought that he made his decision because he was overwhelmed by the glory of God as revealed to him through Nature (which he found a great source of inspiration). But his unconscious motives were deeper and more profound. Did he, for instance, enter in a spirit of humility, with the feeling that, by becoming a minister, he would be able to further the work of the Lord? Was that his real motive?

In view of what we have seen of his character so far, it seems hardly likely. He was not humble, and he had never shown previous signs of awareness of God to any great degree. And there were other considerations to be taken into account.

As a teacher, he had only been able to influence his pupils — those village children we have already met. As a minister, he would be able to influence whole congregations, whole neighbourhoods. And there is also the fact that his flair for the dramatic would have plenty of scope as he took the pulpit to give his sermons. Lastly, of course, a minister would have a much higher social standing than a mere village school-master.

Another interesting fact is that, although it is generally agreed that Patrick was a popular favourite with everyone — he was handsome, and possessed the gifts of natural charm and fluency of speech — he seems to have made no close friends at all in his first twenty-five years. Undoubtedly he was what would be described today as a "loner", and this suggests two things: firstly that he was completely wrapped up in himself and his ambitions; and secondly that his emotions were calculating to the point of coldness.

The only person in Ireland whom he regarded with fondness was his mother, but even when he left for England, his parting message was not "I'll write" (possibly his mother could not read, but she would have been able to get his letters read by someone else). No, he did not promise personal contact, only that he would send money, and though he kept this promise faithfully, he stopped paying as soon as she died.

Emotional coldness does not necessarily preclude the presence of sensuality, however, and the tale of how the young school-master was found in a compromising situation with one of his pupils, a fifteen-year-old red-head called Helen, indicates that Patrick was not indifferent to women. It is indeed probable that there may have been other Helens, for a young man so attractive physically would have found little difficulty in capturing the affections of the local girls if he had cared to.

As we shall see, though, he regarded women as pleasurable diversions rather than as human beings with feelings. Once discovered, he quickly abandoned the luckless Helen. There was no suggestion, for instance, that he might have married her in order to save her reputation — which, after all, had been in his hands, for she was his pupil, and he was six years older at the time, and her teacher.

A more significant point is the fact that at some stage during his teaching career, Patrick had begun to write verse, and he continued to write for most of his life. This aspect of his ambition must obviously be carefully examined in view of the fact that his children were also to write, and to become contributors to the development of English literature.

There are many reasons why people turn to writing. Some see it as an easy way to make money; some have a burning "message" they want to give the world; some wish to impress their fellows — but there are those who are born authors and they write because they cannot help it: they write compulsively.

In Patrick's case, he had no underlying "message" to put forward, no axe to grind. He does not even seem to have been very concerned about the monetary angle, for there is no record of him seeking publication for some time to come, and when he did have his work published, he paid for publication himself.

We know already that he wanted the world to take notice of him, but that alone does not explain his compulsion to write, and the evidence suggests that he was a born author who was driven by some inner complusion to string words together. By his own admission, writing to him was an "indescribable pleasure", and judging from the amount of time he spent writing, it is reasonable to suppose that his other work did not give him anything like the same sense of fulfilment. Writing was, to him, a vocation.

The born artist of any sort, whether writer, painter, actor or composer, is, however, a peculiar species, for if anything should come between him and his work, whether it be a responsibility, a family commitment, a social duty or whatever, warning bells immediately begin to ring. This is the one thing the creative person cannot allow. His work is his life, and to be parted from, or prevented from undertaking, that work, is emotional death to him. Born artists will never accept that any other person or thing should be given priority over what they feel they must do.

Patrick fitted into this catagory perfectly. His writing came before almost everything else (except, necessarily, his church work) and certainly before the feelings and requirements of his wife and children.

Many critics have argued, and are still arguing, about whether Patrick's writing was good or bad. It has been dismissed as worthless; and it has been claimed to be years ahead of its time, and Patrick an educational pioneer. What concerns us, however, is not its quality, but how he himself felt about it. Was he proud of his status as "an author"? Or was he secretly disappointed, his disappointment turning to bitterness, when his works went unnoticed or condemned by the critics? As Thomas Olsen neatly puts it: "The unsuccessful poet or author has all the ambitions, hopes and exultations of the successful writer, with the addition of despair, disappointment and disillusion".

It seems that, certainly in the early years of his career, Patrick was smugly satisfied with himself. He commented that when he was writing his COTTAGE POEMS, "he often reflected that, though the delicate palate of criticism might be disgusted, the business of the day in the prosecution of his humble task was well pleasing in the sight of God, and by His blessing might be rendered useful to some poor soul who cared little for critical niceties".

So obviously, whatever criticism he received left him entirely unmoved, quite certain that, in spite of what the world might think of his writing, his Maker approved of his efforts. This bears out our theory that he was a compulsive writer, for such a person is convinced that he has been put on earth to write, and whether he is successful or not, will carry on writing anyway.

We can therefore add another facet to our emerging picture of Patrick's character. He was (he felt) successful, and this would have strengthened his selfishness and his ambition as well, of course, as his vanity. All writers are vain. If they did not think the world ought to hear what they have to say, they would not write. They may be very charming people socially (as Patrick undoubtedly was) but beneath the polite social mask is a self-centred egotist. Add to that the fact that he was a snob and that he felt himself to be superior to his fellow beings, and we have at least a partial psychological study of the twenty-five year old Patrick as he left Ireland for St John's College, Cambridge.

His years at Cambridge only encouraged these basic qualities in his nature to flourish, for although he had to struggle financially and work hard mentally, he knew that once he had achieved his ambition to become a minister, he would have done the impossible — raised himself from the mud of Ireland to the class of "English gentleman". Now he could afford to let himself make friends — or rather, allow some of his fellow students to make friends with him. For he would need suitable friends and contacts in this new life he was carving out for himself, and, surrounded as he was by young men such as Lord Palmerston and the Duke of Devonshire's heir, he was, he felt, in company with equals.

He did not form close ties with either of these eminent young men, but he did make some friends, and continued to do so as his career advanced. In fact, whenever he was in financial need, kind friends came to his aid, often to a startlingly generous degree. His friends were mostly older men and their wives, or young men like himself, rarely young women. This was only to be expected, of course, for young women in society were not emancipated — but romance was about to lift its head in Patrick's life.

Once having gained his B.A. in 1806, Patrick was ordained deacon, and proceeded to tread his ambitious path by taking up a curacy at Wethersfield in Essex. He was ordained priest at the end of the following year. His next step up the ladder suggested itself quite naturally. He must marry — and marry well — and thus gain a wife of social standing (and, hopefully, some money) to help in establishing the picture he was trying to create of a high-principled Tory gentleman.

We do not know whether he had any dealings with girls, of whatever class, while at college. Very likely not, for his tutors were keeping a careful eye on this slightly more mature student who hoped to enter the Ministry, and would have noted any disreputable escapades. Besides, Patrick had no money to spend on girls, and no time to bother. But now that he was a curate, he could forget hard work, remember that he was tall, handsome and of a flirtatious disposition — and act accordingly.

While at Wethersfield, he proposed to a Miss Mary Burder, wooing her, apparently, with an ardour that swept her quite off her feet. But not, alas, into his arms, for something went wrong, and the marriage never took place. Various explanations for this are available from various sources. People who are sympathetic towards Patrick claim that it was the girl's guardian who parted them. However, in view of what we have seen of his character, another theory which has been put forward seems much more likely: that he was not really in love with her, and his cold, calculating brain decided that though she was suitable enough, he might do better if he waited, and so he jilted her. The evidence of some years later confirms this, and demonstrates how little value Patrick placed on women and their feelings.

He was quite callous in this respect, for when his wife died, leaving him with six small children, he wrote to Mary Burder and in an extremely tactless letter told her that, though she might dislike him (so that even he recognised she had reason to dislike him) his own "love" for her remained unchanged after fifteen years, and he hoped to see again his "dearly Beloved Friend, kind as I *once* saw her, and as *much* disposed to promote my happiness. If I have ever given her any pain I only wish for an opportunity to make her ample amends, by every attention and kindness".

Not surprisingly, Miss Burder sent him a scathing reply where she made reference to his past "duplicity", and added significantly: "Happily for me I have not been the ascribed cause of hindering your promotion, of preventing any brilliant alliance, nor have those great and affluent friends that you used to write and speak of witheld their patronage on my account".

So we can gather from the pen of a lady he had jilted that in the time they spent together, he boasted of what he was going to achieve — and much to her satisfaction, no doubt, proved later that his blinding vanity and ambition had never been fulfilled — and she probably congratulated herself on her narrow escape from being blamed, if she had indeed married him, for his failures.

She absolutely declined to see him, and we cannot blame her, for it must have been obvious, reading between the lines of his letter, that all he wanted was a woman — any woman of position — as a replacement for his wife, to look after his six children and run his house, leaving him free of responsibility. What is quite certain is that his declared love for her did not exist after fifteen years, if indeed, it had ever been there in the first place.

On the breakup of his relationship with Miss Burder in Wethersfield, Patrick left Essex in a great hurry, and put as large a distance as he could between the two of them. He spent less than a year in Wellington, Shropshire, and then was sent to Dewsbury in Yorkshire. From there, he moved to Hartshead-cum-Clifton, where he met Miss Maria Branwell, and made his second proposal of marriage.

We will be examining Maria Branwell

in some detail later, and it is sufficient here to consider Patrick's motives in proposing. Did he really love Maria? Or was this to be another "marriage of convenience" — the convenience, of course, being for Patrick?

Yet again, as in the case of Mary Burder, he proposed within a very short space of time (especially considering the protracted ritual of courtship in those days). But this was a very different lady to Miss Burder. For one thing, she was not eighteen, she was a mature person of twenty-nine. Then again, in Miss Burder's case, there had been her family and guardian to contend with, and guardians were inclined to ask awkward questions about Patrick's family background — which by now, he was ashamed to reveal. But Maria was her own mistress, she could bestow her hand on whoever she chose, and it is clear from her surviving letters that after a month of knowing Patrick, she had fallen in love and agreed to marry him. On her side, certainly, it was a love match.

But what about on his? What would this ambitious and calculating man have gained by his marriage with Maria?

In the first place, he would have obtained exactly what he wanted, a wife of unmistakable birth and breeding who would help him to secure his foothold on the social ladder. It is most unlikely that he would have even considered her as a bride if she had been, say, a servant girl, and not a "lady".

Then there was the question of money. Maria was not an heiress, but she did have a small income of £50 a year. It does not seem much by today's standards, but compared with Charlotte's own Jane Eyre, whose salary at Thornfield Hall was £30 a year, Maria was certainly not penniless.

And Patrick would have found, to his gratification, that though his bride might have been used to handling her own affairs and looking after herself, she was by no means strong-willed, and was only too eager to place herself in his hands, take notice of whatever he told her, and strive her utmost to please him and be a help and not a hindrance. This much we know from her letters.

Did he, then, love her? Let us consider

the evidence. The fact that he kept her love-letters, together with the essay she had written on "The Advantages of Poverty in Religious Concerns" (on which he wrote: "The above was written by my dear wife, and sent for insertion in one of the periodical publications. Keep it as a memorial of her") suggests a sentimental streak we would not have expected in such a self-centred man.

Then when she was dead, the description of his feelings which he wrote to a friend, speaks for itself.

" . . . tender sorrow was my daily portion; . . . oppresive grief sometimes lay heavy upon me; . . . there were seasons, when an affectionate, agonizing *something*, sickened my whole frame, and which is, I think, of such a nature, as cannot be described, and must be felt, in order to be understood. And when my dear wife was dead, and buried, and gone, and when I missed her at every corner, and when her memory was hourly revived by the innocent, yet distressing prattle, of my children, I do assure you, my dear Sir, from what I felt, I was happy at the recollection, that to sorrow, not as those without hope, was no sin; that our Lord Himself had wept over His departed friend . . . "

We must not allow ourselves to be blinded by a natural sympathy for the widower's grief, however. We must remember that we are here to question, to weigh up, and possibly establish, if we can, the real feelings behind his social mask.

Certainly he sorrowed over Maria's death, but there can be other reasons for sorrow mingled with a feeling of loss. Perhaps he may have been moved by her terrible suffering before she died; or (and this sounds more like the Patrick we know) he regretted any hardships he might have imposed on her, for which he could not now atone. Another very common feeling experienced in grief is anger, for the surviving relative or partner is unconsciously angry and resents the departed one leaving him or her to cope. Certainly poor Maria had left Patrick quite a burden — six small children to bring up, feed, clothe and be completely responsible for.

Lastly, to remind us once again of the

character we are dealing with, we will do well to note that the letter to his friend describing his wife's death and his own feelings about it, was later published. Perhaps it was even written with an eye to publication.

Summing up, it is reasonable to assume that when Patrick married Maria, there was an unconscious change in his feelings towards her. His own nature would never have allowed him to love anyone but himself with complete unselfishness, but on marrying Miss Branwell, she became Mrs Brontë, and in his eyes, she became his, an extension of himself. It was through looking at her in this light, through always considering her as "my dear wife" rather than "dear Maria", that he allowed his affection to grow. And he gave her the respect that her position as his wife demanded. She was to him as Caesar's wife, above reproach, a living reminder of just how far he had come in the world.

In this way, then, and in a sensual way (for she was dainty and very feminine) he loved her. But not, we can suppose, with any deep or selfless passion.

Maria Branwell

WE do not know a great deal about this mother of the Brontës. She came from a family that had been established in Cornwall since at least 1605, and was herself one of the eleven children of Thomas Branwell and his wife Anne Carne. Mr Branwell was some sort of merchant, and his wife Anne was the daughter of a silversmith: and the home that they provided for their offspring who survived childhood (for at least three of their children, possibly more, died in infancy) was agreeable and comfortable.

Maria and her sisters were brought up as young ladies. They were educated as befitted their position in Penzance society, though whether they had a governess or attended some sort of school, we do not know. It seems, however, that Maria at any rate took her education seriously, and she emerged from her childhood a cultured young woman who was rather small and fragile in appearance, and not exactly pretty, but who possessed a genteel poise, and quiet good taste.

The story of her meeting with Patrick Brontë, and her marriage to him, can be quickly told, and the facts surrounding this event are almost the only facts that we possess about Maria's life up to this point.

Her parents had died, leaving her with the little income mentioned earlier, and Maria and her two unmarried sisters Elizabeth (later to become the "Aunt Branwell" of Brontë fame) and Charlotte were living together in Penzance when, in 1812, Maria came north to visit her uncle and aunt, Mr and Mrs John Fennell. Mr Fennell had recently been appointed Headmaster of the Wesleyan School at Woodhouse Grove near Bradford, and it seems that Maria was invited to help her aunt out on the domestic front, being particularly good at needlework.

It has also been suggested that Maria came partly as a companion to her cousin Jane, daughter of Aunt and Uncle Fennell, but as Jane had just become engaged to the Rev. William Morgan, and would have been wrapped up in her own affairs, the likelihood is that Maria was intended to act as a sort of unpaid helper to her aunt.

Patrick Brontë was both a friend of William Morgan and an examiner at the school. Naturally enough, he soon met Maria, and the stage was set for their courtship and marriage.

Some sources have it that they met in the June of 1812, others, in August. The one certain fact is that they were married on 29th December in a double wedding with Jane and William Morgan, each clergyman conducting the marriage of the other couple. On the same day, down in Penzance, Maria's youngest sister Charlotte was also married to her cousin, Joseph Branwell. That left Maria's elder sister Elizabeth the only unmarried lady in the family, and as she was by now thirty-six years old, she was probably considered by all to be "on the shelf".

What sort of a person was Maria? We do not have much to go on. In her famous LIFE OF CHARLOTTE BRONTË, written immediately after Charlotte's death, Mrs Gaskell described her in the following words:

"Without having anything of her daughter's rare talents, Mrs Brontë must have been, I imagine, that unusual character, a well-balanced and consistent woman. The style of (the letters she wrote to Patrick) is easy and good . . . " Mrs Gaskell adds: "I do not think that Mrs Brontë ever revisited Cornwall, but she has left a very pleasant impression on the minds of those relations who yet survive; they speak of her as 'their favourite aunt, and one to whom they, as well as all the family, looked up, as a person of talent and great amiability of disposition'; and, again, as 'meek and retiring, while possessing more than ordinary talents, which she inherited from her father, and her piety was genuine and unobtrusive'."

But what exactly were these talents possessed by Maria Branwell? In those days, a woman was not expected to have a gift for business, or anything beyond being decorative and pleasant, and as Maria had never had to run a household while living in Cornwall, it would appear that such talents as she possessed lay in her attractive character and the impression she made upon others.

She was a good needlewoman, that we know; she was not beautiful, but she dressed well, though in a restrained, and not a flashy style. She was probably a good listener, and was tolerant and generous, careful to consider the feelings of others. She may even have allowed herself to be used by less modest and retiring relatives — certainly that would have made her popular, and fits in with the idea of a meek disposition.

The only real evidence we have on which to base our own ideas of her is in the nine letters still extant which she wrote to Patrick before their marriage, and in one short piece previously mentioned, entitled: "The Advantages of Poverty in Religious Concerns".

These have been variously interpreted. It has been suggested, for instance, that Maria as well as Patrick possessed, if not literary ability or aspirations, at least a literary bent: but any girl in love will surely write letters to her fiancé, and it is possible that she wrote her little piece on the Religious Concerns to try and please her betrothed, who she knew was deeply interested in writing. There is no real evidence that she bequeathed any of their mad passion for writing to her children. That, if it was inherited, came from Patrick, who possessed enough for any number of offspring.

So far as Maria's character, as it appears in the letters, is concerned, most biographers of the family mention her as a lady of sprightliness and spirit, well-read, and with a clear mind. Of her genuine love for Patrick, there can be no doubt. She obviously adored him, and expressed her growing affection in terms that were unusually frank for her time. Yet there are inconsistencies in her character that reveal themselves here if we look closely.

Maria tells Patrick in one letter that "For some years I have been perfectly my own mistress, subject to no control whatsoever — so far from it, that my sisters who are many years older than myself, and even my dear mother, used to consult me in every case of importance, and scarcely ever doubted the propriety of my opinions and actions".

It is such remarks as this, no doubt, which have led to the popular picture of Maria as a self-assured and confident person. Yet she freely admits: "I have many times felt it a disadvantage; and although I thank God, it never led me into error, yet, in circumstances of perplexity and doubt, I have deeply felt the want of a guide and instructor". She reiterates again and again in her letters her hopes that Patrick will in the future control her actions and assist her to go forward in life, and expresses constant anxiety that she may not be able to achieve all that he might desire in a "helpmeet" and companion.

This speaks of a distinct lack of confidence, and at least one modern writer, Margot Peters, has had the perspicacity to see that, beneath the light surface tone of the letters, "Besides love, another theme runs through (them) like a troubled whisper: a persistent, morbid self-doubt". We begin to see, then, that Mrs Gaskell was almost certainly mistaken when she described Maria as "that unusual character, a well-balanced and consistent woman". Maria was by no means as well-balanced as she might have appeared.

Margot Peters continues: "Maria Branwell was from all accounts an extremely pious woman. Long years of maidenhood during which her emotions were channelled almost solely into religious feeling intensified the ardent piety of an already religious mind".

This brings us to a second point, which there is no disputing. Even in her love-letters, Maria's piety is evident. She speaks continually of God, often of prayer, and mentions previous "fervent applications to a throne of grace"; she hopes that God will help her to "deserve all the kindness you manifest towards me, and to act consistently with the good opinion you entertain of me — then I shall indeed be a helpmeet for you, and to be this shall at all times be the care and study of my future life".

In fact, as Margot Peters so eloquently comments: " . . . hers seems to have been the piety that breeds as much apprehension as confidence. It is sad to find such an obviously good person feeling abased and unworthy, or brooding on the evils and errors of her heart. This self-doubt enters into her relationship with her fiancé: she is uneasy when expected letters do not arrive punctually: she fancies a coolness in his tone; she asks, 'Do you think you have any cause to complain of me? If you do, then let me know it'." Emotionally, Maria was very much at the mercy of the object of her affection.

Her extreme piety and anxiety over her own goodness, her constant brooding on her failure to be perfect, can be laid in part on the intensity of her upbringing. This same obsession with religion can be observed in her elder sister Elizabeth, when "Aunt Branwell" was living at Haworth and caring for her motherless nephew and nieces. We must conclude that Thomas Branwell's children had been subjected to either an education or, more likely, a home life, which was very strict in moral and religious creeds. This would have affected them all in different ways, according to their personalities, and it obviously drove Maria into an exaggerated conviction of her own unworthiness.

In her letters, we can detect suggestions that, although on the surface she was a self-reliant and capable young woman, in private she had struggled with her innate feelings of guilt and lack of confidence even before she met Patrick, and it is unlikely that marriage to a person of his vanity and self-assurance would have alleviated her earlier opinion of herself.

After their marriage, we hear almost nothing about Maria Brontë. Most biographers of the family have assumed that she was happy — or at least contented — with her lot. Yet this may not have been so. Her letters, though frank in her expressions of love for her future husband, have no element whatsoever of sexual passion in them, and it is possible that, even in the racy period in which she lived, the pious and spiritually minded Maria had very little idea of exactly what to expect from the intimate side of marriage.

She makes no mention of any family that she and her fiancé might have, and the fact that she produced six children within eight years tells us nothing except that she conscientiously performed her sexual duties as a wife. We know, however that for most of those eight years, she was in very poor health, and it is quite possible that her constant child-bearing did not make her happy or fulfilled, but rather the reverse.

To a woman who had prayed that she might be a helpmeet for her husband, a blessing rather than a burden to him, the fact that she often felt unwell, that although she went through the motions of caring for her household, socializing (in the earlier years before the family removed to Haworth, where they had no friends, and knew no-one), she found it difficult in her sickly condition, and that she was unable to be a sparkling and vivacious companion to her vigorous husband, would have only increased her burden of guilt and self-doubt.

In addition, she would have been very aware that each pregnancy meant another mouth to feed, another drain on his resources. Large families were common, but Patrick was not a rich man, and he was not fond of children. A house-turned-nursery was not his idea of a comfortable home, and the probability is that he spent more and more time either shut away with his writing, or out performing his clerical duties. He was not the sort of person to sit for hours consoling an ailing wife.

By the time the family moved to Haworth, Maria was considerably weakened by the bearing of six children, and she had all the difficulties of furnishing and settling into a new house to contend with. Within less than a year, it became obvious that she was dangerously ill, and after an agonising period of some eight months, she died on 25th September, 1821.

If she had suffered before her marriage from morbidness and self-doubt, the history of the subsequent years convincingly suggests that, heavily burdened by feelings of guilt and failure, and emotionally disturbed as pregnant women often are, her lack of confidence and probable depression would have increased rather than eased as time went on. She performed her duties conscientiously while she was able, and loved her children in a gentle, vague fashion — of her love for them there can again be no doubt — but there are hints if we care to look for them, that her life was not one of quiet, peaceful harmony but rather of despair and anguish.

Mrs Gaskell recorded in a letter, for instance, the interesting piece of information that during at least one of Maria's confinements, something went wrong. Taking this and her frail, delicate constitution into consideration, we can deduce that she probably suffered a good deal when all her children were born. She was over thirty when she first became pregnant, and was tiny and slim — not the sort of person who should ever have had children at all.

Mrs Gaskell also tells us that during her last illness, she "used to lie crying in bed and saying 'Oh God, my poor children — oh God my poor children!' continually". Did she fear what would become of them once she was gone, under her husband's far from benign care?

And we do not need to add pathos to

50

the fact (again recorded by Mrs Gaskell) that on her death-bed, the stricken woman would say tremulously: "Ought I not to be thankful that he never gave me an angry word?" But, there are ways other than angry words of inflicting pain and hurt, especially on a sensitive and easily wounded nature.

What, then, was the impression that Maria would have left with her children? Consciously, apart from the eldest, Maria (named for her mother) and Elizabeth (named for her aunt), they could hardly remember her. Charlotte had only the dimmest memory in later years of her mother playing with the baby Branwell in the twilight at Haworth.

Unconsciously, however, they would have retained a sense of gentleness and love snatched away, and it is more than likely that they were aware of her physical suffering as well as her mental turmoil. Perhaps they even held in their minds the unconscious memory of their mother in tears, trying to stifle her sobs lest her husband should hear. And it is extremely probable that in their awareness, but not their understanding, she sowed the seeds of the same self-doubt, morbidity and guilt from which she herself suffered, and which circumstances were later to force to growth in their own lives and personalities.

Her death is generally attributed to cancer of the stomach but in his paper A MEDICAL APPRAISAL OF THE BRONTËS, Professor Philip Rhodes has a different theory. He suggests that "in view of her obstetric history it is probable that her symptoms were related to her pelvic generative organs. It is obvious that she did not die as an immediate result of her rapid childbearing, but probably because of some chronic disorder consequent upon it . . . All in all, I would lean to the idea of chronic pelvic sepsis together with increasing anaemia as the probable cause of her death".

What is certain is that she suffered terrible pain in the months before the end finally came, and biographers paint a touching picture of Patrick spending every spare moment, night and day, with the "beloved sufferer", as he described her in a letter. There are just two points to make that might lead us to suppose that he was not such a comfort to the dying Maria as might appear.

Both were comments made by Charlotte, the child who probably knew her father best. She told Mrs Gaskell that he dreaded a sick-room above all places; and she wrote in another context: "Compassion or relenting is no more to be looked for from Papa than sap from firewood".

Elizabeth Branwell

WHEN Elizabeth Branwell came to Haworth on the occasion of Maria's illness and death, it was not the first time she had been north to visit the Brontës. She was in fact present at the first home her sister had set up with her new husband, Clough House in Hartshead-cum-Clifton, during the birth of Maria's second child, a girl who was (naturally enough) named Elizabeth after her aunt.

At that time, Elizabeth Branwell was thirty-nine years old, and well past her first youth. She was already the same woman, in essence, who would arrive later, at the age of forty-five, to care for the young Brontës at Haworth, and Patrick already knew her well from her first visit, so that her appearance and manner would have come as no surprise to him

Her first visit extended from little Elizabeth's birth in February, 1815, through the family's removal to Thornton, and the birth of Maria's third daughter in April, 1816. This new arrival was named Charlotte after Maria's youngest sister, who had, it will be recalled, been married in Penzance on the same day as Maria and Patrick; and three months after the baby's birth, Elizabeth Branwell returned home.

She did not come north again until 1821, when Maria, now living at Haworth, was on her death-bed. Some authorities claim that she arrived after Maria was actually dead, but it seems more likely that at some point during this difficult period — May, it has been suggested — the distraught Patrick sent for his sister-in-law, whom he knew from experience to be competent and capable (if a little fussy), to run the household and care for the children while he attended to his duties and tried to spend what time he could with his dying wife. And so "Aunt Branwell" became established at the Parsonage, never to leave it until her own death in 1842.

We know nothing about Aunt Branwell's life before she emerged on the Brontë scene. Presumably she had received the same sort of upbringing and education as her sister, and she too was an efficient needlewoman, as the fact that she taught the girls to embroider samplers bears witness. But she had a very different personality to the docile and brooding Maria, and by the age of forty-five, she was an eccentric spinster lady who loved her creature comforts, and whose religious background had bred, not a preoccupation about her own goodness, but a domineering conviction that it was imperative to inculcate in others — especially children — the necessity of duty, self-denial and suffering in order to be saved.

It is notable that Aunt took it for granted that she herself was one of the favoured, and apart from coming to Haworth to nurse her sister and care for her nephew and nieces, there are few, if any, occasions on record when she practised what she preached herself. And even this, as we shall see, may not have entailed such a dramatic sacrifice as might be thought.

The events of her youth are not

recorded except in the stories she was fond of detailing to the people she met in Yorkshire, and naturally, these were strongly biased by her own opinion of herself. Ellen Nussey, meeting the family for the first time when she visited Charlotte after they had left school, wrote later that:

"Miss Branwell was a very small, antiquated lady. She wore caps large enough for half a dozen of the present fashion, and a front of light auburn curls over her forehead. She always dressed in silk. She had a horror of the climate so far north, and of the stone floors in the parsonage. She amused us by clicking about in pattens whenever she had to go into the kitchen or look after household operations.

"She talked a great deal of her younger days; the gayeties of her dear native town Penzance, in Cornwall; the soft warm climate, etc. The social life of her younger days she used to recall with regret; she gave one the idea that she had been a belle among her own home acquaintances. She took snuff out of a very pretty gold snuff-box, which she sometimes presented to you with a little laugh, as if she enjoyed the slight shock and astonishment visible in your countenance. In summer she spent part of the afternoon in reading aloud to Mr Brontë. In the winter evenings she must have enjoyed this; for she and Mr Brontë had often to finish their discussions on what she had read when we all met for tea. She would be very lively and intelligent, and tilt arguments against Mr Brontë without fear".

According to Miss Branwell, then, she had spent her past in a delightfully situated town where there were balls, parties, outings and other activities in which she participated to the full, and where she met eligible young men and — or so she hints — flirted and dallied with them, having large numbers of admirers. This may or may not have been the case, but Aunt Branwell obviously looked back on her younger days with nostalgia, and clung tenaciously to the fashions and habits of her youth, as her taking of snuff, for instance, testifies. She must have delighted in the conviction that she had been a little "fast" or daring, and continued to regard herself in that light, although by the time she came to Haworth, she was in fact slightly pathetic, a left-over figure from a bye-gone age.

Not that anyone needed to waste their sympathy on her, however. She had never married — a circumstance that seems to belie her tales of being a "belle" with a host of admirers — but from what we hear of her character as she appears in the Brontë story, she may have been too headstrong and wilful for a gentleman who wished for a submissive, feminine wife. Certainly she made her presence felt.

As Ellen remarked, she made herself at home in the Parsonage, and carried on a spirited relationship with the head of the household. Daphne du Maurier makes the interesting observation that "the expression in her eyes, shown in an existing miniature, suggests a woman who could easily be clay in masculine hands". Yet one would not have thought that Miss Elizabeth Branwell, who conducted her affairs with such energy, and was convinced of her own importance, could ever have been clay in anybody's hands.

She did not defer to Patrick's opinions, she argued with him. She did not go out of her way to be popular with the servants, she antagonised them. Nancy Garrs, who had come with the family from Thornton, declared heatedly that Miss Branwell was "so crosslike an' fault findin' and so close, she ga'e us, my sister Sarah an' me, but a gill o' beer a day, an' she gi'e it hersel', did Miss Branwell, to our dinner, she wouldn't let us go draw it oursel' in t' cellar. A pint a day, she gi'e us, that were half a pint for me an' half a pint for Sarah". Obviously Miss Branwell felt that servants should be kept in their place, and when it came to the question of the children, it is unlikely that she would have been soft and indulgent towards them, but would have felt it her duty to establish firm discipline in this direction also.

What the children required was an encouraging and loving affection to help them overcome the shock of their mother's death. What they in fact received was a stranger's brisk, no-nonsense insistence on duty and good behaviour, which effectively squashed any attempt on the part of the girls to display their natural emotions, which were seeking an outlet.

Even Mrs Gaskell, whose sympathies lay entirely with the maiden lady who had been forced to uproot herself from her home and take on the tiresome task of caring for a family not her own, admitted: "The children respected her, and had that sort of affection for her which is generated by esteem: but I do not think they ever freely loved her".

Two questions raised by Aunt Branwell's presence in the Parsonage are — what exactly was her relationship with Patrick? And why, if she pined so much for her home in Penzance, did she not return there once the girls were old enough to fend for themselves?

So far as Patrick was concerned, it seems unlikely that there were any sexual undercurrents in their feelings for one another. Patrick's wife had been a dainty, very feminine woman completely different to her sister, and in spite of Aunt's habit of dressing in silk, she does not, at the age of forty-five, appear the kind of person who would have appealed to the sexual instincts of even a sensual man. She was too domineering, too narrow and set in her ways, too wrapped up in memories of a glorious past when she had been a mere slip of a girl. She had discovered that there are other sources of pleasure in life besides romantic dreams — pleasures such as power, independence, the opportunity to follow one's own inclinations. And by this time, Patrick, fast becoming a recluse, was no longer the flirtatious young curate who had fluttered feminine hearts.

Their relationship was that of business partners, no more, who were forced to live in the same house. We cannot feel by any stretch of imagination that when Aunt retired to the best bedroom (which she had appropriated for her own use) and Patrick shut himself in his study to write, there was any yearning emotion in either of them. They enjoyed each other's company, as two people of the same generation in a house full of children, but there is no evidence of more than a mutual respect for each other in any account of their discussions and activities, even if they had not been brother-and-sister-in-law, and had been free to marry.

Having failed in his various efforts to find a second wife, Patrick was more than content for Aunt Branwell to take from his hands the problems of household management and the care of the children. And she, in her turn, quite obviously found the situation to her liking, in spite of her constant bemoaning about Penzance. It is generally felt that she made a supreme sacrifice in leaving the salubrious climate of the south, and that her position in the Parsonage was a trial to a lady of independent means, who might have lived a very different sort of life. But in that case, why did she stay on in Haworth for twenty-one years?

We cannot assume that it was because of any overwhelming love for her nephew and nieces. As we have seen, they respected her out of filial duty, but there was no strong mutual bond of affection between them, and fond through she might have been of Branwell, the only boy, this does not completely account for her long stay in the north.

There must have been something,

however, that kept her in Haworth, and the obvious conclusion is that, when she came to the Parsonage in 1821, she found a whole new life opening up for her — one which suited her admirably, and which she did not wish to relinquish.

Consider her situation in the south. She was the sole unmarried lady left in the family home. Her days of glory were over. She might well have been lonely and bored, with perhaps only a pet to keep her company, and needlework and charity affairs to occupy her mind. But at Haworth, she found that she had all the benefits of marriage, without the inconveniences.

She was plunged into the activity of a household over which she was given unrestricted control. She was allowed to manage affairs exactly as she pleased, and organise everything to her own satisfaction. She did not have to go through the discomforts of bearing children, but there was a readymade family for her to dominate, including a boy, who soon won a special place in her tough old heart.

In addition, she had a distinguished

and courteous gentleman to pay her attention and converse with on familiar terms. It is easy to see that, after lonely days down in Penzance, she must have taken on a new lease of life by finding herself the regulator and controller of a household — and not in any menial capacity, either, but as an honoured blood relation, and not as a mere housekeeper.

She settled in after Maria's death, and found the situation agreeable. And so, she stayed, conscious that in the eyes of the world she was performing her duty on a grand scale. The children benefited from her presence, but they also suffered because of it, so it was undeniably Aunt Branwell who got the best of the bargain.

Nancy and Sarah Garrs

WHEN Patrick married Maria, it is recorded that he engaged "a local woman" to act as the family servant. Nothing is known about this particular woman, not even her name, but it would have been she who assisted at the birth of Maria's first child, and acted as nursemaid to the eldest girl and also to the second daughter, little Elizabeth.

There were plenty of faces to peer into the cradles of these two new babies, for the parents were then living in Hartshead-cum-Clifton, among friends and relatives. Also, as we have heard, Aunt Branwell was staying with the family during this time. And when, after the second baby's birth, Patrick and Maria removed to Thornton, the Brontës had a new visitor, Miss Elizabeth Firth, a young lady who seems to have been fond of children, and who in fact acted as god-mother to baby Elizabeth when the child was christened. In due course, the third daughter, Charlotte, was born.

It was at this point that Nancy Garrs made her appearance in the Brontë household. The "local woman" was probably finding that caring for three infants as well as cleaning, dusting, polishing and cooking was proving too much for her, and an application was made to the School of Industry in Bradford, in order to secure a nursemaid whose duties would lie specifically with the children. Nancy, the thirteen-year-old daughter of a shoemaker, was sent for a trial period.

She was one of twelve children herself, and it is more than likely that she had plenty of experience in caring for young babies. She seemed satisfactory, and so she stayed on as the children's nursemaid. She, in fact, would have been one of the first people with whom Charlotte and the younger Brontës who were yet to be born would have become familiar, and we must therefore consider her as a possible influence on their infant minds and on the development of their future personalities.

Very little attention has been paid to this contribution towards the Brontës' upbringing. It seems that the girls worked hard, Nancy doing her best to run the ever-increasing household, and Sarah keeping the children clean, fed and neatly clothed. Also, they were loyal. When Mr Brontë was appointed to Haworth, the Garrs girls accompanied the family to this remote village uncomplainingly, leaving their friends and the brighter life of Thornton behind them with apparently no regrets.

What we must bear in mind, however, is that these two, who were to care for the children almost single-handed, were very young — scarcely out of childhood themselves. When she first took over her duties with the children, Nancy was a mere thirteen years old, and when Sarah joined her two years later, she was about fourteen. So the main female influence on these baby minds came from two teenaged girls who were by no means "ladies" in the accepted sense of the word.

They were, in the eyes of the family, servants. Mrs Gaskell, in fact, rather patronisingly refers to them as "two rough, affectionate, warm-hearted, wasteful sisters, who cannot now speak of the family without tears". Undoubtedly Nancy and Sarah were fond of the children, and it was from them that the little ones received most of the affection that was given to them in their early years.

But Nancy and Sarah were not well educated, they were practical rather than intellectual or cultured, and although they could dress and feed the infants, they would have been too harrassed and over-worked to do much more than was necessary for the children's well-being. They were not companions, in the sense that a parent would have been a companion; they were young, and naturally more interested in their own lives than in the development of the childish minds in their care. We cannot, for instance, visualise a picture of a quiet family group settled round Sarah's chair as she read to them. What we can imagine instead are the instructions to "Be good, now!"; the occasional slap that would have set the young Branwell roaring; the quick, rough hugs; and Sarah telling the children to "Hurry up, I've got things to do!" It is certain that, warm-hearted and well-meaning though their nursemaid might have been, she would have seemed capricious to them, and had none of the dedication and stability that was the hallmark in later years of a trained English Nanny.

It appears, too, that Nancy and Sarah did not spend all their time with the children. Little Maria, who was a precocious eight years old at the time of their mother's illness, had long since resigned herself to looking after her smaller brother and sisters, and Mrs Gaskell reports, via "a good old woman" who nursed Mrs Brontë, that "the six little creatures used to walk out, hand in hand, towards the glorious wild moors, which in after days they loved so passionately; the elder ones taking care for the toddling wee things".

There is no indication that their nursemaid always accompanied them on their walks, and the inference is that they spent a good deal of time alone, either out on the moors or in the tiny room over the passageway into the house, which was called "the children's study".

We have few other glimpses of Nancy and Sarah in the unfolding history of the Brontës. One fact that has emerged, however, and which we have already touched on, is that the two girls did not like Aunt Branwell. They were happy-go-lucky and indulgent in their attentions to the children, and thought Aunt much too strict.

In 1823, for instance, Maria and Elizabeth both caught measles followed by whooping cough, and were extremely ill. The younger children were infected with a milder form of these illnesses. They, however, were allowed to regain their health and strength by wandering on the moors in the fresh air, but as soon as Maria and Elizabeth were out of bed, their Aunt forced them to sit in her bedroom, with a roaring fire and the windows shut, sewing garments for their proposed departure to Cowan Bridge School, where they had been enrolled as pupils.

Nancy expressed great indignation at this — to her eternal credit — for although she did not know it, such treatment made it possible for the consumption from which the two girls afterwards died to gain a firm grip on their weakened constitutions. Later, Nancy and Sarah reported that Miss Branwell was "a bit of a tyke".

While at Haworth, the two sisters had made their own friends, and during Mrs Brontë's illness, Nancy became engaged. When Mr Brontë heard about it, he went into the kitchen and enquired whether it was true that Nancy was going to marry a Pat. (For her fiancé's name was Patrick Wainwright).

Mr Brontë, as we know, could be charming when he liked to be, and he was the sort of person who always believed in making a good impression on servants. Both Nancy and Sarah were devoted to him (if slightly in awe of his gentlemanly manner). Nancy, rather flustered, answered that, yes, it was true, and that if her Patrick made her a tenth as happy as Mr Brontë had made his wife, then she would consider herself very lucky.

Gratified, Mr Brontë left the kitchen.

It was to be three years, however, before Nancy actually left the Brontë household in order to marry, and the circumstances which brought about her eventual departure and that of Sarah were, as we have seen, their feelings towards Miss Branwell. She, no doubt, was glad to see the back of them, but the children felt differently.

Mama had already gone from them to Jesus. Their father had become aloof and distant. Aunt Branwell frightened them. Were they to lose the two cheerful young faces which had brightened their lives for the last eight years? Were Nancy and Sarah going away for ever?

We can judge how the children regarded their two young nursemaids by the fact that many years later, Charlotte visited Nancy when she was suffering from fever, and, on seeing her former nurse, she burst into tears and ran to kiss her, taking no thought for possible infection. This impulsive act was one of obvious love, not like their dutiful return to England from Brussells when Aunt Branwell was ill and dying.

In fact, both Nancy and Sarah outlived

the girls and their brother, and in later days, when the name of Brontë was famous, they took great pleasure in recalling their association with the family. As well they might, for it was these two who poured a little love into the arid emotional soil of the Brontë children's childhood.

Tabitha Aykroyd

WITH the departure of Nancy and Sarah Garrs, and very probably because of Aunt Branwell's disinclination to employ any further young, chattering and gadding girls to help in the house, Patrick Brontë went to the other extreme, and at some time in 1825, took on a Yorkshirewoman in her early fifties, Tabitha Aykroyd, who was always to be known to the Brontë children as "Tabby". Excluding a short interval of less than three years, she was to remain with the family until a little short of her death some thirty years later.

Tabby has, for some unknown reason, always captured the interest of biographers, from Mrs Gaskell onwards. It is true that she was devoted to the family, and almost became one of them (although, when Charlotte was writing a description of her surroundings in 1829, she mentions "Tabby, the servant", thus letting us see that there was always a certain line of class distinction between them, even when the children were quite young). Certainly she played a large part in the Brontë girls' lives, but she missed those very early, formative years, though her influence was to be evident later on.

We know quite a lot about Tabby, and can gain a reasonable picture of her. She was widowed when she came to the Parsonage, and her maiden name had been Wood. She had relatives in Haworth, but no children of her own, and she had, so we are told, spent some time away from the village. Just before her engagement by Patrick Brontë, she had apparently worked on a farm, but in what capacity we are not told.

It was Aunt who instructed the girls in religious studies, but it seems that Tabby was also very devout — a Methodist — so wherever the girls turned in the house, they came up against a barrier of religion. This was to play an important part in their development, since no single adult member of the household was free from religious prejudices, and these were passed on to the girls, in various forms.

Phyllis Bentley gives us a general

picture of the Yorkshire "type" in her book THE BRONTËS, which will serve as a good introduction to a closer study of Tabby's character.

"By birth," she writes, "they are of mingled Anglo-Saxon and Danish descent. By nature they are robust, practical, sensible, efficient; strongly suspicious of anything excessive in speech, fond of "brass", given to a broad rough humour and independent to the point of perversity. Their secret romance, beneath their practical exterior, is this stubborn freedom, this determined independence, this indomitable tenacity of purpose".

Mrs Gaskell adds to the picture:

"Tabby was a thorough specimen of a Yorkshire woman of her class, in dialect, in appearance, and in character. She abounded in strong practical sense and shrewdness. Her words were far from flattery; but she would spare no deeds in the cause of those whom she kindly regarded. She ruled the children pretty sharply; and yet never grudged a little extra trouble to provide them with such small treats as came within her power. In return, she claimed to be looked upon as a humble friend; and, many years later, Miss Brontë (Charlotte) told me that she found it somewhat difficult to manage, as Tabby expected to be informed of all the family concerns, and yet had grown so deaf that what was repeated to her became known to whoever might be in or about the house. To obviate this publication of what it might be desirable to keep secret, Miss Brontë used to take her out for a walk on the solitary moors; where, when both were seated on a tuft of heather, in some high lonely place, she could acquaint the old woman, at leisure, with all that she wanted to hear".

Tabby was not yet, however, the deaf old servant who insisted on being told of "all the family concerns". She was a lively, bustling, undemonstrative person with a rather sharp tongue, who made sure that, as soon as the girls were old enough to help in the house, they did their share of housework, and were always welcomed in the small kitchen which was Tabby's pride and joy.

It has been claimed that she was far from rough, but was intelligent and refined, although this does not seem likely. Intelligence and refinement are not the same as common sense and shrewdness, and it cannot be assumed by any means that Tabby was on the same intellectual plane as her young mistresses. She may have had a sharp native wit, but she did not favour what would have been known as "society manners"; and her habit of speaking in dialect and using old English words made a distinct gulf between herself and the children.

They were fond of her, kind to her, and regarded her as part of the household, but even she, with her dislike of sentimentality, could not give them the sort of love that would have replaced that of their mother, or set them a model of how "young ladies" behaved. To them she was "a character" with her tales of by-gone Yorkshire days before the industries came, her recounting of grim country superstitions, and her reminiscences of strange and eccentric folk who had lived in the big houses on the surrounding moors.

She was a real and reassuring presence when they gathered in the kitchen on dark evenings, but it is most unlikely that the little girls confided any of their secret fears or troubles to her, in case she should scoff. And so, inevitably, Tabby was completely unaware of the private world to which the children turned for comfort and consolation, deprived as they were of any sort of soft, tender love.

We do know, however, how attached they became to the old woman, and how they appreciated her material care for their wants. When, in 1836, Tabby broke her leg, necessitating special nursing, the girls went on a hunger strike until Mr Brontë allowed her to stay at the Parsonage and let them nurse her. After this incident, Tabby was always a little lame.

In contrast with their Aunt, who never spent companionable evenings with them, but sat upstairs in solitary state in her bedroom, Tabby became a friend — although, of course, she knew nothing of their intense inner lives, or their psychological difficulties. There is something reassuringly homely about Charlotte writing from Brussells that she would like to be in the Parsonage kitchen "watching Tabby blowing the fire to boil the potatoes to a sort of vegetable glue".

Charlotte also wrote to her father, on the subject of Tabby staying on with the family: "It is an act of great charity to her, and I do not think it will go unrewarded, for she is very faithful and will always serve you to the best of her ability; besides, she will be company for Emily".

Comparison of their attitudes will show that the girls were genuinely fond of Tabby, whereas they respected their Aunt only out of duty, but had no real affection for her. Aunt spoke, and they obeyed. Tabby, on the other hand, was a servant, and there could be mutual warmth and sparring between them. Even Emily recorded, in the year when Tabby was seventy five, that she had "just been teasing me to turn as formerly to 'Pilloputate' (peel a potato)".

So from the year when Maria, the eldest girl, was twelve, and the baby, Anne, was about four, Tabby became a family institution. She took her place in the kitchen, and in her brusque, fond way, mothered the children, reproved them, joked with them, and shared their daily lives. Yet we must not forget that, priviledged as Tabby was, she had no understanding of their inner fears and turmoils.

She was not a sensitive woman, and she could not understand the creative nature. Practicality, to her, was everything, and she would far rather see the girls peeling potatoes than messing about and wasting their time scribbling notes on bits of paper. She did not understand the girls' achievements, yet the fact that Charlotte gave her a copy of JANE EYRE when it was published shows that she valued Tabby's approval. They loved her in one way — and she loved them in hers, but their characters and personalities remained a mystery to her.

Tabby was to spend most of her life after she came to the Parsonage busy with cooking and household concerns, and the only significant things that happened to spoil this state of affairs were her several illnesses. Three years after she broke her leg, Charlotte recorded that: "Tabby had to leave us on account of a large ulcer in her leg. She is residing with her sister in a house bought by her savings. She is very comfortable and wants nothing. As she is near us, we see her very often". Two and a half years later, however, she returned, but she was now getting on in years, and we have already heard of her deafness.

Shortly afterwards, she was taken with "a sort of fit", but recovered, although she remained feeble; and a few months after Anne's death, Charlotte found her in a state of collapse on the kitchen floor, unable to move. After this, she was partially paralyzed, yet she lingered on, still at the Parsonage, and it was not until Charlotte, then married to the Reverend Arthur Bell Nicholls, was suffering from her fatal illness that Tabby had to be moved to her nephew's home to be nursed.

She died just six weeks before Charlotte, and, as she would have wished, was buried near the little gate that led from the Parsonage garden into Haworth Churchyard. Even in death, she remained the Brontës' faithful servant.

We should, perhaps just make a passing reference to the other servant at the

Parsonage, Martha Brown, who came as housemaid while Tabby was laid up with the ulcer in her leg. Martha was the daughter of John Brown, the stonemason, and was eleven years old when she first came to serve the family.

She played no part in forming the children's characters, and they did not consult her over decisions, but she remained with the Brontës until Patrick's death, and completes our picture of the inhabitants of that wind-swept stone house at the top of the hill, with the open moors beyond.

Part Two

The Early Years

Introduction

BETWEEN the years of 1813 and 1820, six children were born to Patrick and Maria, five girls and one boy, and in the year of the last child, Anne's birth, the family moved to Haworth Parsonage, where Patrick had been appointed perpetual curate. We have already seen that Patrick was a self-centred man who was concerned primarily with his own affairs, particularly his writing, to the exclusion of everything else. He may well have spared his wife a little of his attention, but it is a reasonable supposition that, in spite of the fact that he is reported to have been popular with young people, he did not care to have anything to do with babes in arms — even his own. He was only interested in his children when they grew old enough to be spoken to as miniature adults — or, as one psychologist has expressed it, "when they were able to argue."

Details of feeding, bathing and nursery routine were not for Patrick, and although he may possibly have handled his first-born, the man who had ignored the births of his younger brothers and sisters at home in Ireland would certainly not have wanted to become involved in such questions as whether little Elizabeth was teething, or if baby Emily Jane had a slight chill. He provided the money for their shelter, food and clothing. Other things could be safely left to his wife.

So the burden of providing the physical love so necessary to the children's well-being fell largely upon Maria Brontë. And, again as we have seen, it is all too likely that, devoted as she might have been to her family, her shoulders were unable to carry the load. Six small children cannot be nursed and cuddled at once, especially by a frail woman often ill, who was continually suffering the discomforts of one pregnancy after another.

Then there were the household affairs to see to, and such social duties as she could carry out, in her increasing frailty. The probability is that, as each child was born, Maria nursed and cuddled it as much as she was able, but it was soon replaced in her arms by the next. And it would not have been at all out of character for Patrick, that cold and calculating man, to order her not to "cossett" or "over-indulge" the children. The likelihood is that they were left to the servants, Nancy and Sarah, who cared for the infants' physical requirements but were naturally unable to provide the love and closeness that should have come from the children's parents.

Even this emotional deprivation might have been overcome, however, if it had not been for the illness and death of Maria Brontë in the year after the family settled at Haworth. She became ill within a few months of their arrival, and had to take to her bed. During the long months while she lay dying, her husband — roused from his preoccupation with himself — spent, as we have heard, his every waking spare moment at her bedside. The children were thus effectively deprived of both mother and father, and by the end of September, 1821, they had lost one parent to death and the other had also removed himself from them. He found their "prattle" distressing; he mourned his wife; he withdrew into his own rooms and into himself. The emotional link, tenuous as it was, between Patrick and his children was completely severed by Maria's death.

This formed, as it were, the first part of the trauma of their early years. The second part consisted of the advent of Maria's sister, Aunt Branwell, who took over the household, temporarily, it was intended at first, but as it turned out, the arrangement became permanent. Aunt Branwell formed the second trauma they had to suffer.

ps

★ ★ ★

The situation, then, was that when Maria, the eldest child, was eight, Elizabeth six, Charlotte five, Branwell four, Emily three, and Anne one year old, their mother's love was taken from them by her death, and that of their father — such as he had spared them — was deliberately witheld. Charlotte, as we have heard, recorded in later life that she could barely remember her mother, and it is almost certain that Branwell, Emily and Anne would not have been able to remember her at all.

All authorities on children's behaviour and development are agreed upon one point — that infants who receive no attention from their parents in the form of touching, physical contact, talk and open displays of affection will grow up emotionally crippled and stunted. Parental love is the first essential of a child's need, and a substitute such as a nurse or a relative, unless completely devoted to the child and in his or her presence continually, can never replace the parents in any satisfactory manner.

Taken to extremes, in communities such as kibbutzes, where children are separated from their parents and cared for by the community, it has been discovered that such children form no relationships with either adults or other children. People mean very little to them, and they have no sense of the value of human life — not even their own. Their values centre around food, clothing and shelter, and they will take enormous risks with themselves, even to the point of virtual suicide, because of their conviction that life is valueless.

The Brontë children were not neglected to this extreme extent, but they were certainly deprived of the love of both mother and father, and as a result, the evidence of stunted emotional growth is clearly visible in their developing personalities. This general fact is quite commonly known and accepted, but it has rarely been analyzed or examined in detail, and this is what I propose to do in this section of the book. Why were the girls literally unable to cope with relationships outside their own home? Why did Charlotte seem like several people — bright and lively within the Parsonage walls, but prickly, aggressive and quick to take offence, yet timid to the point of neuroticism, when in the outside world? Why did Emily reject reality in favour of an imaginative existence? What was the real reason why Anne fell in love with Willie Weightman?

★ ★ ★

Before we begin our investigation of the early years of the young Brontës, one further point needs to be made. Already we have seen that lack of parental love and attention undermined the children at the very foundation of their personalities, making them completely unable to cope with ordinary life. But the lives of this particular family were not ordinary, and we must consider them in relation to their environment.

They lived in an extremely remote and isolated village. They had relatives, indeed, a large number of uncles, aunts and cousins, but they never saw or knew these members of their mother and father's families. They were not encouraged to mix with the local children on a social level or, in their early years, on any level whatsoever. Patrick was a snob. No village children were on a footing with *his* off-spring. His children must keep themselves to themselves.

The result of this was a double isolation and a double burden for these already deprived children to carry. The girls knew no men other than their father and their brother; and no women besides their aunt and the family servants. They never came into contact with "ordinary" children, and so possessed no idea of how such children behaved. This was to cost them dear in later years when they struggled to make a living as governesses — they could not identify with their pupils, and so found that trying to teach young people, an occupation for which they were already temperamentally unsuited, became twice as difficult for them.

In addition, they naturally modelled their own appearance and behaviour upon that of their aunt, and as she was an eccentric spinster who was almost old enough to be their grandmother, their ways of dress and manners — even their hair-styles — were utterly at odds with any social gathering in which they found themselves. Their clothes were old-fashioned and "quaint". Wherever they went, they discovered, to their horror, that they could not help but draw upon themselves that which they most wished to avoid — attention, and occasionally, ridicule.

Little wonder, then, that the four walls of the Parsonage seemed to them a haven, and the world a terrible place full of dragons and dangers which they tried to avoid at all costs. For, even discounting their personality disturbances, the little Brontë girls could never, because of their home background, have been "normal" children, or fitted in in the world in which they lived. They were condemned forever to be strangers in a strange land once they stepped outside the Parsonage walls.

The Developing Child

AT the time when the Brontës lived, no-one had ever heard of psychology in the form we know it today. People had little idea of how their own adult minds worked, much less those of children. And even now, with the breakthroughs of Freud, Jung, Adler and others, we are still exploring and probing. Much remains to be discovered, and a great deal of what is written today is based on conjecture, not proven fact.

However, we no longer have to rely purely on instinct to try and understand a person's character. Certain guide-lines have been laid down for us, and this chapter will attempt to outline how the mind of the average child develops during his early, formative years from birth to puberty.

Some experts claim that the personality of a child begins to develop from the moment he is conceived, and that influences can be felt and absorbed even in the womb. This, however, is far too detailed (and irrelevant) to a consideration of the study of developing minds as we will apply it later to the Brontë children. So too is the theory of the birth trauma. We do not know what happened to the little Brontës at their births or immediately afterwards, neither can we investigate the attitudes of their parents towards each new baby, nor the hereditary tendencies inherited from Patrick and Maria. Such characteristics as were deliberately planted in their conscious minds will be investigated later.

Children do not develop at the same rate — some are quick and bright, others slower, but they all pass through the same sequence of developing processes. We know that this is true of children today, and it is reasonable to suppose that it has always been true of children in our society, although at various periods of history, they were treated very differently to the way they are regarded now, when we are more aware of their development pattern.

The basic difference between the way

modern-day children are regarded and the way in which Victorian children such as the Brontës were treated, lies in the amount of freedom or repression given to their development. The Brontës suffered very much from repression, and this caused them, as well as other children of their time who were similarly treated a tremendous amount of suffering, and prevented them from achieving fully matured and well-balanced personalities in later life.

★ ★ ★

The child passes through at least two states of development — that of the intellect, and the social and emotional aspect. First we will deal with the intellect.

A baby is born with all his senses fully developed, but he has to learn by degrees to use these senses. He is not aware, at birth, that he is a separate entity, nor has he the ability to recognize things or people around him. But by the age of about six or seven months, a baby will know and recognize his mother, and will show signs of distress if separated from her. Memory begins to show itself, and he can recognize familiar faces and familiar things by a year old.

Until about six months, then, the baby is only aware of itself, and does not consciously register separation from the parent, nor any traumatic event occurring around him. After six months, however, both of these can cause distress if they occur, and by the time he is two, the child has learned that he is an individual, and has become familiar with the environment around him.

★ ★ ★

During the ages of about two to seven years, the child learns how to speak and think, but it is important to note that he does not think or reason as an adult would do, and so, as Sula Wolff points out in her book CHILDREN UNDER STRESS, "as a result, he misinterprets his environment. These misinterpretations can cause profound anxiety especially when they go unrecognized by the adults who care for the child, and they lay the foundations for the irrational components of adult personality that persist to a greater or lesser degree in us all."

Sula Wolff reports that Piaget, the great pioneer of child behavioural psychology, asserts that there are four main characteristics of the years two to seven: firstly, the child lives in an egocentric world where, though he can communicate with others, he thinks and speaks only of things with which he himself is concerned, cannot imagine that other people have any other interest but in himself, and regards himself as the literal centre of the universe.

The second characteristic is that everything that happens in the world around him is caused by things — even inanimate objects — feeling and thinking just as he does.

"There are no impartial, natural causes for events," writes Sula Wolff. "All explanations are psychological in terms of motivation and every event occurs by intent . . . At this stage, children believe in magic and words are as powerful as actions. Children cannot yet dissociate the word from the object it names nor the thought from the things thought about. The psychological and the physical world are one. Dreams really happen and good and bad wishes can quite possibly come true."

From this, it will be seen that a child's logic at this stage is quite different to the logic of an adult. Children will accept explanations that do not make logical sense, and do not try to puzzle out the truth. Anything they cannot understand, they assume must be "magic".

The fourth characteristic laid down by Piaget is that, to children under seven, a rule is a rule, and must be obeyed without question. Even if they do not always obey the rules, they have no doubt that they are in the wrong, and the rules are right. An interesting example is given by Sula Wolff of this idea of "authoritarian morality" when she points out that "the crime begets the punishment".

"If a five-year-old disobeys his mother," she writes, "by running into the street and then falls over, he fell *because* he was naughty."

And so, to the child at this age, all bad things happening to him are likely to be viewed as punishment, and (because of his idea that he is the centre of the universe) it is punishment for something that *he* has done wrong — even though he may have no idea what it is, and may in fact have done nothing at all. All things that occur are seen by him as being rewards or punishments for whether he has been "good" or "bad". This will be an important point when we come to consider the traumas that beset the little Brontës, and how they attempted to cope with the difficulties they encountered in their early years.

The ordinary, average child next passes through a stage where the beliefs, as detailed above, gradually fade and he becomes aware of real logic, is able to make deductions from his own observations, and form a co-operative attitude to others. He has, by the age of about twelve, begun to grow into an adult, thinking person.

★ ★ ★

This is the intellectual development of the child, but there is also an emotional side to his progress, which concerns the fears and anxieties that arise from his childish views about himself, the world, and what is happening around him. The first seven years are, as we have seen, the most important in this respect, for not until he has passed through the stages just described does he become able to think or act rationally.

Even an "ordinary" child is quite likely to suffer from fears and patterns of behaviour that linger into adult life from the first seven years, and when we consider the occurrences in the lives of the little Brontës, we can see that their early years were far from "ordinary", involving traumas and difficulties which none of them managed to overcome successfully.

These will be dealt with more fully, and individually, at a later stage. It is enough at present to say that all of them suffered, to a greater or lesser degree, from anxiety arising from those early years, and which influenced them as they grew to adulthood, and beyond.

★ ★ ★

Anxiety, fear, discomfort, are the first feelings a new-born baby knows. It is expressed from a safe and secure environment within the womb into a world that is full of "foreign and doubtless terrifying extremes of cold, roughness, pressure, noise, nonsupport, brightness, separateness and abandonment" — to use the words of Thomas A. Harris.

This is physical birth. Within a few moments, however, the baby's "Psychological Birth" takes place (again according to Harris) when someone reassures the baby that life is not all frightening. Warmth, support, and the act of physical touch or "stroking" — which we mentioned at the beginning of this book as so necessary to the baby's psychological well-being — are provided, and the new baby begins to feel that living isn't so bad after all. From then on, however, the child's life is a constant battle against such a feeling of desperation and aloneness occurring again.

The baby is dependent on others — usually the mother — for food, warmth and the love and expressions of love so vital to its survival, and in its early months, when it is helpless, it will show its anxiety by crying if deprived of food, warmth or love, until what it requires is provided.

Various experts have different theories on the nature of anxiety and its causes in the growing child. Ian D. Suttie, for instance, follows up his views that the child is dominated by an overwhelming need "to retain the mother — a need which, if thwarted, must produce the utmost extreme of terror and rage, since the loss of the mother is, under natural conditions, but the precurser of death itself."

Suttie conjectures that the need for the mother is later transferred into a need for general companionship, and also speculates on the emotions of anger, even hatred, which can occur if mother-love is witheld. One point he makes is worthy of note. Along with Harris's insistence that "stroking" or touch is necessary for an individual's psychological well-being, we find Suttie stating that "it is long before the child completely outgrows the need for bodily contact. Even many adults retain the need for caresses apart from sexual intentions and gratifications."

And most experts would agree that there is a very devious web of fear, anger and hate mingled with a baby's or a growing child's love for its mother or its parents.

* * *

Sula Wolff expresses things much more simply. She asserts that during the child's first year of life, its anxiety springs mainly from deprivation of biological needs. In the second year, however, when a child is expected to begin to learn civilized manners, and how to behave, "anxiety . . . springs from shame" (when the child is scolded) "and the disapproval of others".

We are now entering upon those vital years between two and seven, when, as we have seen, the child has many difficulties in its intellectual growth.

On the emotional side, too, there are changes. The child must begin to fit into a group consisting firstly of his family — mother and father and brothers and sisters — as well as into social situations.

Strange and unpleasant new emotions can arise, such as jealousy and rivalry. The child must learn that his immediate wants cannot always be satisfied; that there is a future, and certain things must wait. It is at this point that the youngster begins to compare himself with other children, and to learn how to model himself on his father (if a boy) or her mother (if a girl). At this age, also, sexual and erotic emotions concerning the parents develop for the first time.

Naturally, children at this age are curious about everything, but they find that some of their questions, especially concerning sex, seems to embarass their parents, and this not only deepens their curiosity, but makes them feel it is wrong to ask about such things.

Another source of anxiety presents itself at this time, with the beginning of a developing conscience. Their conscience reminds them of all the things they have been scolded about, all the things they have been forbidden, and we must remember that, since this is the period when, as Sula Wolff puts it, "thoughts are as powerful as deeds, when morality is harsh and authoritarian, when crime begets punishment", feelings of guilt can be overwhelming, and can cripple a child for life.

★ ★ ★

Until he is about twelve, the child continues his learning process of finding out about the world about him and exploring himself. He has to fit into his social environment, and learn how to get along with other children of his own age. He will perhaps discover that he is brighter, duller, quicker or slower, than they are. He makes conclusions about himself as a personality.

These conclusions will, if the child has managed to survive his early years successfully, culminate in the formation of a well-balanced identity during puberty and adolescence. But even the luckiest, happiest child will almost certainly possess unresolved problems lingering from his early years, and the teenager is given, as it were, a second chance to sort them out, as they surface once again.

Few are able to achieve a complete mastery over these problems, and any children with particular difficulties — such as the young Brontës — need especial help. As we know, such help was not available to them at the time when they lived, and so they passed into adulthood permanently affected by the traumas and troubles of their early lives.

★ ★ ★

This, very briefly, is an outline of the development of the average child of our society. It is by no means complete, and we will be adding further details as we proceed to investigate the children individually.

I propose to consider the children in two different stages as well as examining the characteristics and personalities of each child. Firstly, as a group of six, and later, after the deaths of Maria and Elizabeth, as a group of four. Our next chapter, however, will deal with Maria and Elizabeth, their positions in the family and their particular problems and development.

Maria and Elizabeth

(i)

MARIA, the eldest of the Brontë children, appears, from the evidence of Mrs Gaskell, Charlotte, and everyone else who has recorded anything about her, to have had four main characteristics: she was devoted to her sisters and brother; she was good to the point of saintliness; she was intellectually precocious; and she was chronically untidy. In fact, she was the perfect child, except for the endearing untidiness, and this in itself is suspicious. There is no such thing as the perfect child. It has been pointed out by William James, the American psychologist, that the healthy young child is a pagan, and pagans, as we all know, are not unselfish and saintly.

We must therefore examine Maria's character a little more deeply to discover the real feelings and emotions which lay beneath her outward behaviour.

Her devotion to her brother and sisters, so great that she unhesitatingly took over the role of "Little Mother" when their own mother died, can be interpreted in quite a different way to an ordinary child's casual fondness for her family. Maria apparently never quarrelled with anyone, she was always calm, kind, understanding and unselfish, and put her brother and sisters first, and herself last.

This is unnatural behaviour, and in order to try to find out the reason why she showed such intense devotion to her little flock, we must go back to the year 1813, when she was born. From her birth until that of Elizabeth in 1815 — that is, some year and a half later — Maria was an only child, and was no doubt petted by all the friends and relatives who lived near them or came to visit. She probably also enjoyed a happy and loving association with her mother who could at this point spare time for her first-born.

But within the next six years, Maria found herself pushed out of her priviledged position in order to make way for five new babies, all of whom demanded her mother's attention. Her natural reaction would have been intense jealousy of these squalling strangers who had taken her mother's love away from her, as well as alienated her father, who might well have spared his first-born a little of his attention, but who shunned a nursery full of babes in arms and toddlers.

Maria's feelings would have been extremely complex. By all accounts she was an unusually bright child, and the indications are that she possessed a strong personality. We must also bear in mind that, while the new babies were filling up the nursery in close succession, she was entering that important phase between the age of two and seven. She was egocentric, and her jealous thoughts to her were as powerful as any bad actions would have been. In addition, the loss of her mother's devoted attention and her father's interest were likely to have been interpreted by her as some sort of punishment for something she had done wrong.

Let us, then, consider Maria's position. She felt that the loss of attention she received was due to her own badness.

She began to hate her mother on two counts — firstly because, as Suttie puts it, "Earth hath no hate *but* love to hatred turned, and hell no fury but a baby scorned"; and secondly because she was at the stage of development where she was in love with her father, and wanted a relationship with him which would exclude her mother.

But set against this the fact that in the Brontë household, it is very likely that even as a young baby, Maria had an unusually over-developed conscience. Her mother was pious and would have seen to it that as soon as she could speak, the little girl learned to fold her hands and lisp her prayers, and she would have heard her father talk of God and his wrath against the wicked. And so to herself, she must have seemed very wicked indeed to wish bad things against the new babies, to hate her mother, to want to take all her father's attention for herself.

The sense of guilt, anxiety and fear would have been too much for her young mind to bear, and so she protected herself by pushing all her natural feelings, emotions and conflicts into the level of her unconscious, where she was completely unaware of them. This is a common method of psychological defence when the natural instincts of the personality are incompatable with the voice of conscience, and to Maria it would have been unbearable to admit to her real thoughts and feelings.

As she had not achieved a satisfactory progress through the difficult two-to-seven stage, she can also be said to have become "fixated" in this childhood period — it would need to be properly dealt with in her mind before her personality could progress further emotionally, and, in her case, she did not live long enough ever to be able to deal with it.

Another form of defence mechanism used by Maria was that of "reaction formation", where an individual's real feelings and emotions become turned into the opposite. She was, in reality, jealous of her brother and sisters, but instead of showing her jealousy, she went to the other extreme and became their champion, their passionate defender against all odds, their second little mother. This links up with her real feelings towards her own mother. It was unthinkable to hate her mother, but by becoming her mother's helper, by always being good, by assisting with the younger children, she could show, in her conscious behaviour, how loving and happy she was to be able to be of assistance to her ailing and over-worked parent.

Even more complex, however, is the fact that by acting as "Little Mother", Maria's real feelings were showing through her self-protective mechanisms, though she was unaware of this. She was unconsciously trying to take her mother's place, and push her mother from the family group. Equally unconsciously, she pursued her erotic feelings towards her father by trying to gain his attention in subtle ways.

We have already mentioned that one of her main characteristics was her intellectual precocity and this was a direct (though unconscious) bid to draw her father's interest and attention to herself. Patrick believed, as the evidence of his own childhood shows, that education was the great stepping-stone that led to social advancement. He had no time for emotional links with his children, but he admired intellectual prowess, and Maria set herself to win his approval — we could even call it "intellectual stroking" in place of "physical stroking", using Harris' word for interaction between parent and child — by becoming intellectually brilliant in a way her father would appreciate.

Mrs Gaskell herself unknowingly gives us evidence of this.

"'Maria would shut herself up' (Maria, but seven!)" she writes, in the words of the old woman who nursed Mrs Brontë, "'in the children's study with a newspaper, and be able to tell one everything when she came out; debates in Parliament, and I don't know what all'."

But alas! Poor Maria's efforts did not have much affect on Patrick's flinty heart. He may have given her a word or two of praise, he even commented proudly to outsiders that he was able to talk to her about the events of the day as though she had been an adult, but in the main, his attention was focussed on his boy, Branwell, and there were none of the cosy walks alone with Papa, herself holding his hand, for which Maria longed.

We may argue that this was not her purpose at all, that she was simply a precociously brilliant child, but the evidence of the teachers who examined her work when she went to Cowan Bridge School gives no indication of this extraordinary brilliance she is supposed to have possessed. Her report on entering the school recorded: "Maria Brontë aged 10 . . . Reads tolerably, writes pretty well. Ciphers a little. Works (needlework) very badly — knows a little of Grammar. Very little of Geography or History. Has made some progress in reading French, but knows nothing of the language grammatically . . . " Naturally, the teachers would not have dreamed of enquiring whether such a young child was able to absorb and discuss the contents of a newspaper, debates in Parliament and all, and as far as general education and capabilities were concerned, Maria made a rather poor showing.

★ ★ ★

A difficult and complex character, Maria constantly bore the anxiety engendered by the conflict between her conscious and her unconscious. She must often have felt that she wanted to scream her jealousies and her frustrations to the world, but her conscience had firmly shut the door of her mind on any display of resentment or anger (to her, that was "wicked"), and so Maria's pattern of behaviour never varied. She was always good, always loving, always obedient, always willing to serve and assist the other children and her mother. And — most dreadful of all — always conscious of an innate sense of unworthiness and wickedness in herself, which she could not understand, but which was ever-present.

This brings us to her fourth characteristic, her chronic untidiness. Most habits or ritual behaviour, if taken to excess, have some psychological basis behind them, and, unable even to know why she was doing so, Maria felt that somehow, she deserved to be scolded, even punished, for her inner wickedness. She knew she would not be scolded for her "ordinary" behaviour, so her unconscious mind devised a scheme which would bring down the disapproval of her parents and associates upon her — she became chronically untidy.

If we read JANE EYRE, where Charlotte used her sister Maria as a model for the character of Helen Burns, we will see how Helen was punished, scolded and made to suffer for being constantly untidy. Mrs Gaskell, too, tells us that:

"One of these fellow-pupils of Charlotte and Maria Brontë, among other statements even worse, gives me the following: — " and goes on to describe how one morning, Maria, who had been ill and had to have a blister applied to her side, felt too unwell to get up, and was urged by the other girls to stay in bed. But, martyr-like, "the sick child began to dress, shivering with cold, as, without leaving her bed, she slowly put on her black worsted stockings over her thin white legs (my informant spoke as if she saw it yet, and her whole face flushed out undying indignation). Just then, Miss Scatcherd" (one of the mistresses who particularly disliked Maria) "issued from her room, and, without asking for a word of explanation from the sick and frightened girl, she took her by the arm, on the side to which the blister had been applied, and by one vigorous movement whirled her out into the middle of the floor, abusing her all the time for dirty and untidy habits. There she left her. My informant says, Maria hardly spoke, except to beg some of the more indignant girls to be calm; but in slow, trembling movements, with many a pause, she went down-stairs at last — and was punished for being late."

Maria never complained at such treatment — partly because her unconscious had clamped firmly down on her natural impulses to become angry — she had long since forced herself to be "always good"; and partly because she felt, again unconsciously, that no punishment could be strong enough to wipe out the badness she felt inside. She was a child who carried a heavy burden of psychological difficulty, and it is quite likely that, even if she had not died so young, she would have spent a lifetime searching in vain for the love of her mother, which had been taken away from her by the advent of her brother and sisters, and the notice and approval of her father, which she would never have obtained. She would also have continually punished herself.

★ ★ ★

As we have mentioned previously, Maria was a strong character. Although she lived for only a few short years, the impression she left upon the rest of the family, and on everyone who had known her, was outstanding. An interesting point here can be quoted from a psychologist who told me: "Deprived children tend quite often to be, amongst other things, domineering".

We shall later be considering other aspects of deprivation in connection with the other young Brontës, but in Maria's case, we have already seen how, quite unconsciously, she fought for domination of the other children with her frail and ailing mother. She became the leader of the little family — and we shall hear more of this in the next chapter. Mrs Brontë's death would therefore have affected Maria in a different way to the rest of the children. She would have triumphed inwardly — and again unconsciously. Now she was *really* the "Little Mother", the one to whom the others turned. Her hold over the rest of the children was complete. And yet, all had been achieved by an outward show of quiet saintliness and unselfish love.

A person with such psychological difficulties might have been expected to have suffered from illness — quite often ailments are brought on by the extreme anxiety of conflict. But Maria has no record of nervous illness. She was, perhaps, a frail child, and we know that before going to Cowan Bridge School, she and Elizabeth (and indeed, the other children too) were stricken with measles and whooping cough. Previously, it is also recorded that during Mrs Brontë's last illness, all six children suffered from scarlet fever. But these were ailments that swept through the whole family, and did not centre on Maria alone.

It was not until she was actually at Cowan Bridge that we hear of Maria suffering from some unspecified ailment where she had to have a blister applied to her side — and this might well have been due to the onset of the consumption which, aggravated by the dreadful conditions at the school itself, killed both her and Elizabeth.

On 14 February 1825, Patrick went to bring his sick daughter home. She was nursed at the Parsonage by her Aunt and the new servant, Tabby, but to no avail. She went into a decline, and showed no will to live — though her resignation to her fate was taken, by those about her, to be a saint-like desire to be with Jesus.

John Lock and W. T. Dixon comment, in A MAN OF SORROW, that: "There was no need to pray for her, as she rarely ceased to supplicate for her own salvation". To us, this suggests interesting possibilities. We know of Maria's exemplary conscious behaviour. She would certainly have felt that she deserved to go to heaven — and yet, beneath the surface, all her sense of badness and wickedness, her conflicts and anxieties and fears, were festering in her unconscious. She had done bad things, she had taken her mother's place, she was unworthy, she was doomed, she was damned!

It is very likely that, with her resistance lowered, Maria's other self, the dark centre of her unconscious, was crying out for relief from her inner torments, and she did nothing to help herself in the course of her illness.

Poor, bewildered, frightened Maria's traumas were gently put to rest for ever when at length she died on 6th May. She was twelve and a half years old. Thus ended the life of one of the most complex personalities of the Brontë family — though even in death, her influence was to be far-reaching.

(ii)

It is impossible to attempt a psychological portrait of Elizabeth, the second Brontë daughter, for so little is known about her. Like Maria, she was born while Mr and Mrs Brontë were living at Hartshead, and the family was surrounded by relatives and friends. Shortly after her birth, the couple and their two babies moved to Thornton, where other friendly faces would have welcomed the little Elizabeth — in particular, that of the spirited young lady who made such a fuss of the Brontë children, Miss Elizabeth Firth.

Miss Firth in fact became the child's godmother, along with the children's aunt, Elizabeth, "Aunt Branwell", who, as we have recorded previously, had come from Penzance to visit her sister. In the years that followed, it is possible that little Elizabeth remained Miss Firth's especial favourite amongst the children.

She must have been either a happy-natured child, or especially shy, for there is no record of her ever saying or doing anything particularly memorable. Only on three occasions can any mention be found of her, and she seems to have lived very much in the shadow of her more domineering sister Maria.

The incident of the mask, where Patrick questioned all his children as they hid their faces, is the only occasion on which we hear the voice of Elizabeth. Patrick's question to her was, "what was the best mode of education for a woman", and her answer: "That which would make her rule her house well", shows that here was no budding feminist, no ambitious mind dissatisfied with a woman's position in the scheme of things, but a modest nature whose main hope in life was to be a good wife and mother.

Perhaps Elizabeth was the most "ordinary" of all the Brontë children. Certainly she was no frustrated genius, and seems to have possessed few, if any "hang-ups". Not that we must read too much into her reply from behind the mask, for all the children (except Emily) gave the reply they thought would please their father. They had other masks behind which their real natures were hidden.

Elizabeth's next appearance in the Brontë story is when she accompanied Maria to Cowan Bridge School. She and her elder sister had for a short time been sent to the school at Crofton, near Wakefield, the one which Elizabeth Firth had attended, but little seems to be known of their stay there, and they were quietly withdrawn, possibly because Patrick could not pay the fees.

The record of Elizabeth's entry at Cowan Bridge reads: "Elizabeth Brontë, aged 9. (Vaccinated. Chicken pox, Scarlet fever, Whooping cough.) Reads little. Writes pretty well. Ciphers none. Works (needlework) very badly. Knows nothing of Grammar, Geography, History or Accomplishments." Certainly it appears that Elizabeth had not striven, as had Maria, to improve her education and please her Papa!

It was while at Cowan Bridge that a mysterious incident occurred concerning Elizabeth. The headmistress later wrote to Mrs Gaskell: "The second, Elizabeth, is the only one of the family of whom I have a vivid recollection, from her meeting with a somewhat alarming accident, in consequence of which I had her for some days and nights in my bedroom, not only for the sake of greater quiet, but that I might watch over her myself. Her head was severely cut, but she bore all the consequent suffering with exemplary patience, and by it won much upon my esteem . . . "

Whatever could this "alarming accident" have been? We can only guess, and the headmistress gives nothing away.

But then, as soon as Patrick had removed Maria to the Parsonage to die, it became obvious that Elizabeth was seriously ill with the same complaint, and the poor child was hastily sent home in the care of a motherly lady, Mrs Hardacre. She left the school on 31st May, and two weeks later, on 15 June 1825, she was dead at the age of ten.

Her short life had passed immemorably, and if it were not that she bore the magic name of Brontë, it is doubtful whether this little girl would ever have achieved mention in the history books — or indeed, in any books at all.

Tragedy

THE seven years after Maria's birth, while Mrs Brontë was bearing her other five children, were comparatively easy for the little ones. Maria was early in developing her unnaturally "good" behaviour pattern and carrying her burden of unconscious guilt and anxiety, but Elizabeth was cheerful and uncomplicated, and the four youngest had not really encountered any of the severe traumas which were to come.

As each child was born into the family — which was then resident at Thornton — it would gradually have become aware that the love of Mama, though genuine, was but a fragile thing, unable to be relied upon, and that Papa was a far-off and stern figure with whom it was impossible to make loving contact. Thus the children did suffer from a sense of deprivation in the home, and this would have implanted in all of them a feeling of basic insecurity.

A child needs a stable atmosphere and the supportive love of its parents equally given however many children there may be, and each one requires to know that its mother and father love and cherish it as an individual, with no favourites, so that each may feel secure to face the world. In the Brontë family, there was no stability for any of them — except that Patrick was beginning to show a leaning towards his only son — and every one of the girls began to suffer from an insecurity that was later to become chronic. It is important that we remember this basic insecurity, however independent or self-sufficient the children's behaviour may have appeared on the surface in later years.

But while they were at Thornton, they had a mother — remote and aloof though she was — who was pretty and fashionably dressed; they had the rough affection of Nancy and Sarah Garrs, and they had contact with the outside world, particularly with spirited young Miss Elizabeth Firth, who was fond of these well-behaved little creatures, and often invited them to tea. It would have taken only a small amount of affectionate petting and coaxing on her part to have the children forgetting the manners their Papa drilled into them so sternly, and to have them running about, chattering and giggling and playing games, like any ordinary little group. We can be almost certain that times were not altogether unhappy at Thornton.

But in 1820, the year of Anne's birth, a series of events began which left the children crushed, bewildered and unable to remember a time when they had ever known the carefree delights of childhood. In that year, first of all, the family moved to Haworth. All the familiar scenes and friendly faces of Thornton were snatched away, and they were installed in a strange house with only the presence of Nancy and Sarah for comfort. They were not allowed to try and make friends with the village children, for as we have already heard, Patrick was a snob, and he instilled into his off-spring the conviction that they were "a cut above" the urchins who tumbled merrily up and down the village street. No, they must not speak to the impudent children of the village. Surely they could amuse themselves with better things.

But even while they were beginning to settle into their withdrawn existence and take a certain amount of timid pleasure from exploring the garden of their new home and the surrounding moorlands with Sarah, further storm-clouds were gathering. Their Mama, always frail and wraith-like, took to her bed, and as the weeks passed, they saw nothing of her. "She was ill, very ill", they were told, and Nancy and Sarah were constantly warning them to be quiet for fear of disturbing the invalid. Mama became a ghost-like figure shut away in her sick-room upstairs. Papa grew sterner and more unapproachable than ever, and they took care to keep out of his way, scarcely understanding what was taking place, but knowing only that something dreadful was happening.

They heard talk they did not fully comprehend — talk of death. What was death? Was Mama going to go away and leave them for ever? Would they never see her again?

Much has been made of the fact that at this point, they behaved in a docile, unobtrusive and quiet manner. Such behaviour from a group of youngsters is again not natural, and we must conclude that, as well as the fact that, in the manner of the day, their Papa would have made strictly clear to the older ones what sort of behaviour he expected from them ("Children should be seen and not heard"), they were cowed by the sudden move to a strange place, and their insecurity was fast increasing as they watched their father's movements about the house and listened to the moans from Mama's room with frightened eyes. Their unnatural quietness came about not because they were "good", but because they were afraid, wild little creatures terrified by the unknown and scarcely comprehended happenings around them, clinging to each other — and especially to Maria — for safety and security.

★ ★ ★

It might be as well for us to consider at this point the ages of the children during the year 1821, when their mother was on her death-bed. Maria herself was a precocious and domineering eight-year-old who was only too ready to gather the younger ones under her wing and provide them with a focal point to which to cling. Her power over the little group was greater than ever, and her unconscious mind was triumphant because now, the little ones were giving her all the love they would otherwise have been giving to their Mama. They would not stir from her side, and they followed her around everywhere. To them, she was the breath of life itself, and Maria encouraged their dependence upon her.

Elizabeth was six, and almost certainly her sister's faithful admirer. Charlotte, at five, was just beginning to cope with interpersonal relationships, and was wrapped up in her egocentric preoccupation that all these bad things that were occurring must in some way be her fault. She, more than the others, leaned on Maria for comfort.

The only boy, Branwell, was too young, at four, to comprehend what was happening, and knew only that the attentions he had previously received from his father had suddenly stopped, or were reserved for the invalid upstairs. Emily was three, and both she and the year-old Anne were simply distressed and bewildered by the disappearance of the loving presence they knew as their mother. Their minds had not yet come to grips with the traumas that were besetting the family.

★ ★ ★

At this period, another attitude was added to the children's basic insecurity — a feeling of inferiority. They had all (except perhaps Anne and Branwell, who was his father's pride and joy) discovered to some extent that their Mama found them a burden, and their Papa had no time for small girls. Maria, beneath her outward composure, was very aware of her inner unworthiness; and Elizabeth could not understand what she had done to be ignored by her parents. Charlotte was rapidly coming to the conclusion that there must be something very wrong with her for so many bad things to happen, and felt that however hard she tried to please, she could never earn praise or loving support from those in authority. She, in particular, suffered from a chronic state of inferiority brought on by the neglect of her parents. Emily was three, and was just entering the important two-to-seven stage. What happened to her then and in the next few years would have a vital effect upon her developing personality.

Into this atmosphere, fraught with tension and anxiety for the children, came a stranger whose presence only intensified their feelings of inferiority. She swept into the Parsonage, ready to criticise, organise and interfere, a lady, old to their young eyes, who was sharp and forceful, their "Aunt Branwell" who, they were told, had come on a long journey from a far-away place called Penzance to help to nurse their sick Mama and to take care of them.

Maria and Elizabeth had seen her before, but to the young Brontës she brought only dismay and a realisation of just how many faults they possessed. When she was not in Mama's sick-room, she was criticising Nancy and Sarah, their rough but loving links with happier times, in the kitchen, or tut-tutting over the children's bad habits.

An older group of children would have formed a mental existence of their own in defiance of her, but at this point the children were too young to organise themselves into a real group, as we know it. Susan Isaacs, the child specialist has, however, pointed out that even small children may group themselves together in defiance of adults as that way they feel safer, and we can be certain that the older girls, at least, clung round Maria to try and off-set the feeling of insecurity that Aunt Branwell engendered in them. Branwell was bewilderedly torn between his love and loyalty to Maria, his "little Mother", and the petting that Aunt showered upon him — for she indulged him and made him her favourite — while Emily copied her sisters, and Anne, the baby, was still much too young to take any part in defensive action.

It was not in Maria's nature to defy authority, however. She had to be good, and she encouraged the others to withdraw rather than try and establish themselves as individuals. The children kept out of the adults' way as much as possible. They spent a great deal of time alone in "the children's study", where Maria told them stories and taught them what little she knew. And we have already seen a picture of them walking on the moors, hand in hand, the two eldest taking care of the little ones. Aunt approved of such quiet, docile behaviour while there was sickness in the house, and the unnatural, unchildlike pattern that would govern the rest of their childhood years became established. They withdrew into themselves.

Kingsley Davis in HUMAN SOCIETY makes the point that an individual lays great importance on the attitudes of other people, especially their approval or disapproval, and he adds: "It is only through the approval of others that the self can tolerate the self."

If we apply this to the little Brontës, we will see that in their eyes, their very existence seemed to bring about disapproval all around them, in all the adults in the family. Even Mama did not want to have them near her any more.

And so, in order to overcome the terrible burden of inferiority and insecurity this situation precipitated, they had no-where to turn but to each other.

They could tolerate and love each other — but outside their little childish world, no-one else, it seemed, could tolerate them at all. So although they gave lip-service to the demands of Papa and Aunt, and allowed themselves to be warily fond of Nancy and Sarah, the six children were undergoing the beginning of a change. Their world was shrinking to encompass only their own six personalities.

No-where else could they find a generous, open-hearted love — so they turned to each other for affection. And as time went on, they became convinced that to outsiders, they were unloveable. We shall see later how they tried to cope with this conviction as each one grew older.

In September, 1821, Mrs Brontë's months of suffering came to an end with her death. To the children who had been estranged from her for so long, the blow would have been lighter than might have been expected, especially as, so far as we know, the custom of the period was not followed in that in this case, they were not brought in to kiss their Mama and bid her a last goodbye. One wonders why this custom was not carried out, but it is possible that her illness had so ravaged Maria Brontë that even Patrick and Aunt recognized that to see her would be too much of a shock for her young children to undergo.

The same unexpected thoughtfulness is evident in the fact that only the two eldest girls, Maria and Elizabeth, were present at the funeral a week later. The younger ones were only told that "Mama had gone to Jesus", but as they watched from the window of "the children's study" and saw the coffin being carried out, and Nancy and Sarah Garrs in tears, they must all have felt that something very precious had gone from their lives for ever, and they clung even closer to each other, too stricken by anxiety and apprehension even to weep.

★ ★ ★

After this series of major traumas, the children were given a brief respite before the next lot of blows fell upon them. Mrs Brontë died towards the end of 1821, and until the middle of 1824, some two and a half years later, a quiet settled over the Parsonage. The children were in some measure able to try and come to terms with what had happened to them, little realizing that even greater trials were to follow. Some biographers paint a sentimental picture of Patrick and Aunt settling into a peaceful routine of teaching the children and generally taking them in hand, but this omits to mention certain facts, and what we can deduce from our knowledge of the characters of all concerned.

Aunt had come to Haworth in a temporary capacity only, and probably planned to return to Penzance after her sister's death, so some other person must be found as soon as possible to take her place as chatelaine and be responsible for the children. They were unaware that, if events had gone the way Patrick planned, they might have had a step-mother, and their story might have taken a different turning. For after the first edge of his grief at his wife's loss had blunted (and as soon as he decently could) Patrick became very much occupied with the prospect of marrying again, and as early as the end of 1821, he made his first proposal of marriage to try and replace Maria — this was to none other than Miss Elizabeth Firth, who had been so fond of the family when they lived in Thornton.

She, however, refused him, but he set about making other proposals, and we can be reasonably sure that the question of his re-marriage and the pursuit of his clerical duties probably occupied his mind to a much greater extent than the teaching of his children. Aunt, too, was expecting to be told at any moment that she would soon be free to return to Cornwall, and was probably beginning to make her own plans.

So the likelihood is that on the whole — at least for the first year or so after their mother's death — the children were left a good deal to themselves, and received little formal education but for what they gave each other, or discovered for themselves. Many writers about the family have praised Patrick's liberality of thought in making no restrictions on what his children were allowed to read, but we must remember that, going back to his own childhood, he had known what it was like to have to educate himself, and how books had excited him and fired his imagination. So, with his own childhood in mind, he allowed the children the freedom of what books the house possessed. He had begun by reading adult works, so why should they not be permitted to do the same? He wanted them to be well-read — and he himself was the supreme example of a self-educated man constantly before their eyes.

During these months, then, they helped each other. The little ones were taught to read and write, and the children browsed amongst the books on the parsonage shelves and discovered their own favourites, without being burdened with formal instruction. One of their favourites was probably Bewick's HISTORY OF BRITISH BIRDS, which Charlotte mentions in some detail in JANE EYRE, and we know that at some stage, whether then or later, the children were greatly influenced by the works of Sir Walter Scott and Lord Byron, as well as country ballads and old legends. Books can, and have been written on the works which they probably read during the course of their childhood, but the exact details of these do not concern us at the moment. It is sufficient to say that their education, though unusually broad for children of their particular ages and era, was erratic, to say the least.

When Patrick eventually gave up his hopes of being able to re-marry, and Aunt accepted the fact that she was not going to return to Penzance, then some effort was made to supervise the children's education. Lock and Dixon tell us that Patrick "instructed the eldest of the children himself", and he was probably dismayed to find how little they knew of such subjects as mathematics, geography and history. However, he had been a teacher, and knew how to set about putting things right. The same book adds that he also taught Maria Latin and politics, but in her entry to Cowan Bridge, no mention is made of her having any knowledge of these subjects. Possibly she was not questioned on them, for they were unusual in a young girl's education.

Dixon and Lock also add that Patrick was aware of the genius of his children even at this early stage, and place the incident of his questioning them behind a mask as having occurred at about this time. Yet again, as we have already mentioned, no signs of unusual talent were discovered when the children went to Cowan Bridge, and no mention is made by the headmistress of her recalling the family because of their extra-ordinary brilliance. We can therefore conclude that Patrick, who wrote of this incident some thirty years later to Mrs Gaskell, was allowing later events to influence his memory. As I have previously pointed out, each child gave an answer to Papa's questions which — in their child-like knowledge of their father — they knew he would approve and applaud.

We are told that Aunt supervised the younger ones, Emily, Branwell and Anne, and a point that must be raised here is

Aunt's attitude to religion. We already know that she was a strict Methodist and that she felt it her duty to warn others of the sins of the flesh (she herself being one of the "saved"). Later we shall see that it was this seed of guilt and unworthiness, planted so young in her conscious mind, that caused Anne a great deal of suffering, influenced the character of Emily in a way that Aunt could never possibly have imagined, and weakened the personality of the already basically weak Branwell.

The religious upbringing they received was to prove a hazard to all the children, and as Sprott points out in HUMAN GROUPS, early influences will shape the personality of the infant so that it rarely accepts a new and completely different set of standards, morals and so on, without a struggle in later life. Even the attempt to conform can bring feelings of guilt, as if we are betraying something. So the concepts of morality and duty which were drilled into the children in their early years never left them, though they struggled later to avoid the guilt feelings that overcame them when they tried to break the code Aunt had instilled, or else they called into play various unconscious defence mechanisms.

Another seed planted even earlier in their young minds was the attitude of their father towards themselves and other people in general. Outwardly a good and pious minister — even, it may be remarked, unusually conscientious in his duties — he was still inwardly, as we have seen, filled with a sense of superiority and scorn for others, which he transmitted unknowingly to his family. He was unable, however, to pass on his own individual personal charm (now slightly faded) and his self-confidence, and so in the children, the superiority and snobbishness absorbed from him often came into conflict with the feelings of inferiority and unworthiness they had gained from his neglect and the circumstances of their early lives. Again and again, we shall see this happening, especially clearly in the character of Charlotte, and to a lesser degree, of Branwell.

Cowan Bridge

IN 1823, a new trial beset the children — that of separation from each other. As previously mentioned, Maria and Elizabeth were sent to a select girls' school, and we can imagine the dismay this caused all of them. But after a few months, when no doubt the two elder girls found themselves completely out of their depth among a group of "young ladies" who had known the benefit of happy, secure homes and possibly governesses, Patrick was forced to withdraw his daughters, and what joy there would have been in the Parsonage when the six children were united once more.

However, the prospect of school was still uppermost in their father's mind, (though to the children it was far more important that they should all be together) and as all Brontë lovers know, the new school for Clergy Daughters at Cowan Bridge seemed to Patrick an answer to prayer. Here, his girls could be educated cheaply, and fitted for future positions in life as governesses or teachers — the only course that he would have considered suitable for females of his daughters' standing — unless, of course, they married. But to the lad from the cabin in the wilds of Ireland, a good education was essential. Consequently, the girls were enrolled as pupils at Cowan Bridge.

It seems to have been taken for granted that young Branwell, the only boy, should be privately educated at home, although one wonders why, for in those days, education and a good school was far more common amongst boys than girls. Branwell would need to be able to earn a living as well as, possibly, provide for a family if he were to marry and have children.

However, when the girls were preparing to go to Cowan Bridge, Branwell was only seven years old, and his father, a trained teacher, no doubt felt that he was quite capable of dealing with the education of his only son for the present. Later, perhaps, a good school could be considered.

So yet again, the girls' lives were turned upside-down. In addition to the fact that they were all going to be sent out into a frightening and alien world, Nancy and Sarah were about to leave the Parsonage, and the children clung desperately to their dear nursemaids, trying not to cry at the thought that they would never see their two only friends any more.

Aunt scoffed at such foolishness, no doubt. She would be glad when the girls were off her hands, especially as she had just had to cope with an outbreak of measles and whooping cough amongst all six children, which had delayed Maria and Elizabeth's departure for Cowan Bridge. One wonders just how much of Maria and Elizabeth's illness was aggravated by psychological reasons, brought on by the memory of their previous attempt to go to school at Wakefield.

But at last they were ready to leave, and the girls consoled each other that at least they would be together again once they were all at the school. Maria and Elizabeth left Haworth in July, 1824, and Charlotte was sent to join them in August. Emily followed in November, and now only Branwell and the four-year-old Anne were left at the Parsonage in the care of the new servant who had replaced Nancy and Sarah — Tabby.

It is at this point that we must broaden our canvas a little and consider the four eldest girls not in the confines of the Parsonage walls, but coping as best they could in the very different atmosphere of a girls' school. Even allowing for the fact that Charlotte may have exaggerated in JANE EYRE (although she always maintained that she had not, and most experts today agree that the conditions at Cowan Bridge were, to say the least, highly unsatisfactory for young girls, especially the Brontës, who were just recovering from illness), their lives at Cowan Bridge were practically unbearable, both mentally and physically.

They were made to suffer cold and hunger; and, already carrying their burdens of psychological problems, they found that they were also humiliated and constantly reminded by the Rev. Carus

Wilson, the administrator of the school, that they were vain, unworthy and unloveable creatures, born into sin, who were being educated by charity. They should be meek, he maintained, and humble, grateful for the "blessings" being bestowed upon them.

Maria, as we have seen, accepted everything with bowed head; and Elizabeth probably struggled along as best she could, but with many a secret tear. Emily, who was the youngest pupil (then aged six) did not suffer as much as the others, for she was, according to the headmistress when the latter wrote to Mrs Gaskell: "quite the pet nursling of the school", and the older girls would have made much of her. But Emily had already shown signs of the way in which her personality was to develop, and she was not influenced either way by the favourable treatment she received.

It was Charlotte, already emerging as as strong a character as Maria in the family, on whom Cowan Bridge left the greatest impression. She was, it is interesting to note, recognized as being of a particularly bright intellect, for the record of her entry reads: "Charlotte Brontë (8) . . . Reads tolerably. Writes indifferently. Ciphers a little and works neatly. Knows nothing of Grammar, Geography, History or Accomplishments — Altogether clever of her age, but knows nothing systematically . . . "

All told, Cowan Bridge was the most shattering experience Charlotte had yet undergone, even surpassing her mother's death, and in addition to her feelings of insecurity and inferiority, the aggression which is often present in deprived children began to rear its head, although Charlotte's conscience and habit of self-control forbade her to express it openly. But it was there, raging in her eight-year-old heart as she suffered herself and watched Maria suffer. Years later, she was to record that rage and rebellion in the pages of JANE EYRE.

★ ★ ★

It is the natural instinct of young children to seek love — particularly the love of their parents. Only if they know they are unreservedly loved can they give love in return, and deprived children find it difficult to love. They are, to quote my psychologist friend, inclined to be "overdemanding, or suspicious, or hostile, or domineering".

We have already seen that Maria was domineering, and now Charlotte, the deprived and rebellious eight-year-old who had lost the love of her mother and hardly known the love of her father, displayed signs of suspicion and hostility towards any kind of affection from an adult. She and the others had already banded together and turned against Papa and Aunt — and not without reason. Margaret Howard Blom comments crisply that Patrick was "clearly unfitted" to give his children "a fostering maternal love" and Aunt regarded her care of them as "an onerous duty". We have already discussed how much of Aunt's presence at Haworth was an "onerous duty" to her — but certainly she did not regard her fostering of the children as a labour of love!

So the children were already on the way to a feeling that the world consisted of "Them" and "Us" even before Cowan Bridge. This episode, to Charlotte, confirmed that feeling for the rest of her life. "They" had scolded and punished Maria, her beloved, meek, gentle sister, and driven her to her death, and for that, she would never forgive "Them".

It became one of the facets of her personality that she found it difficult to love anybody outside the family circle of her brother and sisters. This applied in some measure to females, but particularly to males, with whom she had learned no point of contact. And yet, she craved love. As we shall see, her attitude towards love was to cause her a great deal of distress and misery in later years.

But it was not love that she sought from "Them" at Cowan Bridge now — it was too late for that. Power was what she desired — power to avenge what had been done to herself and her sisters. Power to be authoritative, to be able to do things, to manipulate others, as she herself had been manipulated, power for its own sake. She wanted to be somebody important — anybody except the insignificant little Charlotte

Brontë. If she could have pulled down Cowan Bridge brick by brick and burned the ruins, she would have done it. This desire for power, too, was to haunt her for the rest of her life.

★ ★ ★

By the end of June, 1825, Maria and Elizabeth were dead, and the rest of the children were home once more, the devastated Patrick having rushed to Cowan Bridge to remove Charlotte and Emily. Philip Rhodes gives it as his opinion that "From the evidence, scant as it is, it is possible that Maria and Elizabeth died of pulmonary tuberculosis which disseminated in the form of miliary tuberculosis." But whatever the cause, they were dead and buried, and it is worth mentioning here that Maria's death was to have a disastrous effect upon Branwell.

He was almost eight years old, and scarcely understood the nature of death, but, in accordance with the custom of those days, he was held up to kiss his eldest sister as she lay in her coffin, and the image of her dead face shocked his whole system. For the rest of his days, he was never to forget dead Maria, and it can truly be said that she haunted him. The others grieved for their lost sisters in their own various fashions, but Branwell had been stricken to the heart by his first vision of death, and it was never to leave him, but to weave a morbid theme through all his thinking and writing until the end of his life.

What effect did the death of the two eldest girls have upon the other children? We must pause here to consider a child's view of death, for children do not view it as an adult does. The passing of their mother had taken place at a distance, removed from them, as it were, for they did not see her in her coffin, nor witness her burial, and all they knew was that a gentle, tender presence had slipped for ever from their lives. But with Maria and Elizabeth, it was different. The two girls had been near to them in age, and Maria had been their "Little Mother" for as long as most of them could remember. One might have expected them to be overcome with grief.

But in 1825, Charlotte was nine,

Branwell eight, Emily seven, and Anne five. In simple fact, the children were all too young to comprehend fully what death meant, for it is not until about the age of nine that a child is able to understand death in a rational and logical way.

Sula Wolff sums up the child's reaction to death as follows: " . . . children react to death as our knowledge of their intellectual development would lead us to expect. Under the age of about four or five they ignore the phenomenon or else respond with puzzled and somewhat callous interest. Between five and eight they become intrigued with death, associating it with aggressive feelings and fears, regarding it as a punishment for misdeeds but also as reversible. It is not until they are about nine years old that they acquire a rational comprehension of death. It is at this age also that sorrow begins to be expressed in response to the death of a loved person. Before then children often do not react emotionally at all or else they merely take a detached interest."

It is unlikely, therefore, that the

surviving Brontë children were prostrated with grief at the deaths of Maria and Elizabeth. They simply accepted the fact that their sisters had "gone to Heaven". However, they had all suffered the loss of two parental female figures, their mother and their "Little Mother", and this would have had an effect on their own identity formation patterns. Particular distress was caused in Emily, as we shall see later. Also, of course, the loss of their loved elder sisters would have added to their feelings of insecurity.

* * *

For the next five years, the four children, Charlotte, Branwell, Emily and Anne, remained living quietly at the Parsonage. We have already seen that even before Cowan Bridge, the children had partly withdrawn into a "Them" and "Us" situation, and during this period, their withdrawal became complete, and further foundations were laid for the formation of their characters. They became a psychological group, defined by W. J. H. Sprott as "a plurality of persons who interact with one another in a given context more than they interact with anyone else. The basic notion is relatively exclusive interaction in a certain context".

People form groups for all sorts of reasons — sometimes because they have interests in common, or because they work together. The little Brontës, however, though they also fitted into the group of the household, knew that there was no supportive love to be looked for from Papa or Aunt (though they spent a certain amount of time with each, doing lessons, or sewing, for instance) and they withdrew psychologically into a Group that was exclusive to them mentally, driven because they needed love, and only by forming their own little circle were they able to survive in an otherwise loveless house. In their insecurity, and overcome by feelings of inferiority, they turned to each other for love, companionship and support.

This was a different sort of group from the original one made up of the six children before Cowan Bridge. Then, the disparity in their ages and the fact that Maria and Elizabeth had ruled them as "Little Mothers" had made them a gathering under a definite leadership, the little ones leaning upon their elders. Now, as the five years at home passed, they become more of an age, and their Group was a psychological social entity where each had their own individual part to play, uniting them into a cohesive whole.

The Group

THE children formed themselves into a Group in order to find love and companionship, without which they could not survive in their particular environment. They would have come to know each other and their personal opinions and reactions very well indeed, for of course, they were still individuals in themselves, but, as Sprott points out: "The group, if it has been in being for a time, assumes a kind of independent existence in the minds of its members."

Charlotte, Branwell, Emily and Anne would have regarded themselves as "We" or "Us" and the rest of the world or the people they knew as "Them". Even Tabby, though they came to love her, was never allowed to become one of "Us", though she, and even Papa, were sometimes given a glimpse of some of the Group's activities.

Charlotte later wrote, in a letter to

Henry Nussey, what their Group meant to her — and to all four members. She did not, naturally, realise that this was in fact what she was doing, but she was actually defining the importance the Group had upon influencing and shaping the Brontë children's future personalities when she wrote:

"My home is humble and unattractive to strangers, but to me it contains what I shall find nowhere else in the world — the profound, the intense affection which brothers and sisters feel for each other when their minds are cast in the same mould, their ideas drawn from the same source — when they have clung to each other from childhood and when disputes have never sprung up to divide them."

Philip Rhodes acknowledges the existence of the Group and its unnatural aspect in his medical appraisal of the family, with the following words:

"The tragedy of the Brontës resides in the isolation, begot by the peculiarities of their father and by the death of their mother when they were young. The deaths of Maria and Elizabeth drove them further inwards upon themselves and they had very little support from adults, and indeed may have rejected it.

"It can only be said that in similar circumstances the majority of people would not have responded in quite such an extreme fashion."

But here, we must point out that we are dealing with one particular group in one particular environment, and the whole purpose of this book is to examine why and how the Brontës became such strange and odd individuals. We have already seen that these were extremely deprived children, in the sense that they received, as Harris would have expressed it, no "stroking" from their parents — or at any rate, not enough to justify a healthy psychological existence. Their mother was now dead, so was their "Little Mother", Maria, and their father was authoritarian and gave them no emotional support whatsoever, although he could occasionally make a gesture — as in the case of the famous box of twelve wooden soldiers which he brought as a present for Branwell, with other little gifts for the girls.

He encouraged their mental development and, so we are told, spent a fair
amount of time teaching and conversing
with them, thus continuing the intellectual
"stroking" which poor Maria had received.
Aunt, too, gave praise for good work
where it was due, but they received
no warmth, no physical contact, no
touching, and as we have heard from
various authorities, touch is a necessary
part of human expression of feeling
— and lack of a loving touch can
cause an individual intense distress as
he searches to find it.

The girls were even barred from
sparking off physical contact with their
father themselves, and not waiting for
him to initiate it. They may at times
have wanted to show their father that
they loved him, but the lack of their
mother as a model made it difficult
for them to know how to express their
feelings — their insecurity would have
feared to meet with rejection — and
because they were never spontaneous in
their ways by, for instance, throwing their
arms around their father, he became even
more of a remote figure, and the problem

went round in a vicious circle.

So the five years after Cowan Bridge went quietly by and the Group gained in power and authority over the children's minds and developing personalities. They found the love and affection they sought with each other. Charlotte speaks sentimentally of the fact that disputes had never divided them and their minds were "cast in the same mould". As a matter of fact, their minds were not cast in the same mould, they were four very different personalities and the only things they possessed in common were their deprived background and their need for love. But, as Sprott points out, the Group would have assumed an independent existence for them, and as they grew, the fact that they were "We" or "Us" became in certain respects more important to them than their own sense of personal individuality.

Within the Group, then, they could function effectively as social beings. They could be unselfconscious, they could express themselves, they could talk without fear of criticism or rejection, they knew that each of the other members loved them and valued them for themselves. They approved of each other, and to quote Kingsley Davis again, "It is only through the approval of others that the self can tolerate the self."

In addition, they found a way of obtaining Harris's "stroking" within the Group. It is unlikely that Papa or Aunt ever touched the children or gave them any physical caresses, but when they were out together on the moors, for example, they could hold hands and feel physical contact with other human beings. Their physical closeness lingered long into their later life, and whenever they were together at the Parsonage, the girls would walk round and round the parlour table in the evenings with their arms about each other's waists, discussing their writing and the events of the day.

It was also remarked upon by Ellen Nussey that Emily and Anne were "like twins", and obviously these two felt the need for physical closeness, even if not actually touching each other. Philip Rhodes comments that "the whole family was neurotically inturned upon itself and unable to make realistic contacts with the outside world."

There was no one "mother figure" in this Group, as there had been with Maria, but it was only to be expected that a dominant character would emerge as a leader whenever anything had to be done. Inevitably, the dominant figure grew to be Charlotte, who had already felt the taste for power. Yet in these early years, she did not command.

She and Branwell, who was conscious of his importance as the only boy, were the two eldest, and it was both of them together who initiated what was to become the whole *raison d'etre* of the Group — no less than a massive piece of psychological defence mechanism on the part of all four of them: the creation of a fantasy world in which they could act out their fears and aggressions and escape from their burdens of insecurity and inferiority, guilt and fear. And — even more important — in this fantasy world, they could find love.

* * *

169

It is through play that a child channels its anxiety and any disturbing emotions or aggressions it may feel, away from itself. Play is therefore very necessary to a child, but there were various reasons why the little Brontës did not have the opportunity — or indeed, the inclination — for happy childhood games in their early years. They had too many traumas to cope with, they had Maria giving them the lead in the importance of "being good", they had Aunt constantly telling them to be quiet, they had Papa repeating that education and reading were more important than anything else for a growing child. Because children who are playing are usually noisy, disruptive and argumentative, ordinary childish games had no opportunity to develop between them, and therefore in their repressed, docile, unnatural quietness, they bottled up their tensions aggressions and fears. We can consider two points here. When Charlotte went later as a pupil to Miss Wooler's school at Roe Head, one of the girl friends she made there, Mary Taylor, wrote later to Mrs Gaskell: "In our play hours she sat, or stood still, with a book, if possible. Some of us once urged her to be on our side in a game at ball. She said she had never played, and could not play."

So here we have evidence that Charlotte, at least, had never learned how to play as a child. All her interest had gone into her reading, or, later, her writing.

On the other hand, we have Emily's slap-dash diary note written in 1864 when she was sixteen and Charlotte had returned from Roe Head. The future author of WUTHERING HEIGHTS scribbled:

"I fed Rainbow, Diamond, Snowflake Jasper pheasant (alias)" (these were some of the family pets) "this morning Branwell went down to Mr Driver's and brought news that Sir Robert Peel was going to be invited to stand for Leeds.

"Anne and I have been peeling apples for Charlotte to make us an apple pudding and for Aunt nuts and apples Charlotte said she made puddings perfectly and she was of a quick but limited intellect. Tabby said just now Come Anne pilloputate (ie pill a putato) Aunt has come into the kitchen just now and said where are your feet Anne Anne answered On the floor Aunt . . .

"It is past Twelve o'clock Anne and I have not yet tidied ourselves, done our bedwork or done our lessons and we want to go out to play . . . "

We can see from this that Emily's spelling and grammar were atrocious for a girl of sixteen, but her mention of going out to play does not mean that she and Anne were about to indulge in childish games. "Play" to them at this stage in their lives meant scrambling on the moors, wandering together in their fantasy world.

★ ★ ★

It was the year after Maria and Elizabeth's death that the Group's creation of their fantasy world began, and as they grew, so their fantasies changed and grew with them. The story of how they began to "act out" little dramas is too well known to give here, and it is sufficient to say that in the beginning, Patrick was aware (and possibly even encouraged the children, remembering how he too had declaimed verse aloud as a young boy) that Charlotte and the others invented small dramas of their own around the persons of the wooden soldiers, and even wrote tiny books about the activities of their main characters.

But what Patrick did not realize was how deeply involved, how withdrawn into fantasy, the Group became. Their imaginary lives soon became more important to them than reality, as they realised that the dramas or "plays" they enacted in their heads, and the tiny books they wrote about the adventures of their characters, could give them freedom from their real-life insecurities, fears and anxieties.

Soon, their writing, which took up all their spare time, began to be kept secret from the adults. They could not wait to get mundane daily chores over with so that they could escape into the world of Glasstown — Charlotte and Branwell's early creation, a kingdom on the African coast — and Gondal, Emily's separate kingdom, which she introduced to Anne while Charlotte was away at Roe Head.

So during these five years the children

spent together at home, the foundations were laid for a more sophisticated form of play — intellectual and literary — which was to prove so potent that Branwell and Emily never escaped from its clutches, and Charlotte, recognising the dangers of this drug-like fantasy in later life, had to make a supreme and heroic effort to break free of it. Anne was not quite so deeply affected, but she had her own problems to cope with.

★ ★ ★

The "juvenilia" — for such is the name given to the thousands of words the children wrote about their fantasy worlds — was the most important single factor in their youth. They covered the pages of tiny books only a few inches in size with microscopic print which kept their work secret until a hundred years later, when an American scholar, Miss Fannie E. Ratchford, undertook the monumental task of trying to collect, decipher and piece together the many fragments. She reported in her famous work THE BRONTËS' WEB OF CHILDHOOD that the series of histories, stories, dramas and poems suggested not the popularly accepted picture of frail, gaunt, nervy children, but happy spirits with a magic lamp which could take them anywhere in time and place, so that they could mix with emperors, and assume God-like importance.

Undoubtedly it was the juvenilia that gave Charlotte and Emily the opportunity of learning their craft as writers, so that when they came to write their mature works, they had already served a long and arduous apprenticeship, and were by no means beginners. But how did the creation of Glasstown (Angria, as it later became) and Gondal and the "magic lamp" affect their psychological development as people?

Sadly, their involvement in the fantasy world was to prove a great burden to them. Already withdrawn into their Group, they would have found, once they realized that Glasstown gave free rein to their imaginations, that they possessed less inclination than ever to try to make contact with reality. Their heroes and heroines were far more real and more important to them than any ordinary human beings they came across in the mundane business of day-to-day living, and the colour and glamour of their imaginative settings made the real world seem dull by comparison. So as well as their personality defects, they now had an extra obstacle to overcome in their attempts to live normal lives.

Summing up, the events and deprivations of their early years, from babyhood to adolescence, had brought them insecurity, chronic anxiety, and an inability to cope with interpersonal relationships outside the walls of the parsonage and the protection of their Group. Their fantasy world brought them a good deal of mental stimulation and enjoyment, but prevented their ever finding their own identities and becoming balanced personalities. The girls made heroic efforts to cope with the demands made upon them by the events of their later lives — how far they succeeded we shall see in the later parts of this book.

Part Three

Charlotte

Charlotte

(i)

BEFORE the family moved to Haworth, Charlotte was a bright, interested child of quick intelligence who, under different circumstances, might have become a spirited and fulfilled personality in later life. Because of what happened to her at the Parsonage, and the events that clouded her young years, however, this promise did not materialize, and, as Philip Rhodes comments:

"In (her) psychological reactions she must be classed as neurotic, and the manner of her later death to some extent bears this out."

We must first of all, then, examine as well as we can what is meant by the term "neurotic". Philip Rhodes adds that: "A neurosis is characterized by an over-reaction to surrounding circumstances, and over-react she certainly did." Another psychologist has put it to me that a neurotic person "is forced to make excessive use of defence mechanisms because their everyday experiences are so far out of step with the person's self-concept. The individual goes further and further away from the real world, and is never able to discover for himself (or herself) his own identity."

The basic motivation for ordinary living is the ideal regard of others. One wants to be approved, to be admired, and especially to be loved — particularly, in the case of a child, by one's parents, and all the little Brontës suffered from a deprivation of parental approval, admiration and love.

Charlotte's "case history" began when the family moved to Haworth, and her mother was taken ill. She was then five years old. Already she had discovered to some extent that her mother had little time to spare for her, and her father none at all. She was strictly brought up, as were all the children, and was expected to behave herself and exert a good deal of control over her natural childish feelings of ebullience and curiosity about the world. Now, with her mother ill, the family was forced to be even more quiet and well-behaved, and her eldest sister Maria set them an example in self-denial.

Charlotte was in the throes of coping with the two to seven period when she was egocentrically convinced that she was the hub of the universe, and everything that happened was because of her. If it was good, it was because she had been good; if it was bad it must be her fault for being naughty.

Her mother's illness and the fact that they had been moved to this strange, unfriendly place, were both very bad things, and Charlotte became convinced that it must all be her fault in some way she did not understand. As we have previously seen, she suffered more than any of the others from a feeling of inferiority that verged on the chronic, brought on by the deprivation of her parents' love and the occurrences at this particular time in her life. Aunt Branwell's advent did not help to alleviate this sense of inferiority, and Charlotte clung to the loving and understanding Maria for support.

It is difficult to know just how deeply her mother's death affected Charlotte. An interesting book by Robert Keefe, CHARLOTTE BRONTË'S WORLD OF DEATH, puts forward the theory that the little girl felt guilt and self-hatred after Mrs Brontë died, and was convinced she had murdered her mother. We already know that Charlotte suffered from deprivation at the abandonment by her parents, and Keefe agrees with this.

"Abandonment," he writes, "was both Brontë's greatest personal fear and the central motif of all her fiction."

I personally do not go along, however, with his further theory that Charlotte possessed a death-wish in order to compensate for the "murder" of her mother, and that "Both Brontë's art and her life can be seen as a struggle against her will to die."

If we look at her months at Cowan Bridge, we will see that the headmistress passed on to Mrs Gaskell her recollection that Charlotte had been very talkative, and that she remembered her as a "bright, clever little child". So neither her mother's death nor the neglect of her father had yet succeeded in cowing Charlotte's early natural ebullience.

Maria's death, however, was a different matter. By this time, Charlotte had fostered her rage and rebellion against "Them", the authorities at Cowan Bridge, for her own treatment there, and that of her sisters. She was nine when Maria and Elizabeth died, probably able to appreciate their deaths rationally, and to grieve over such a waste of young life.

She was not crushed, though, by the dreadful sorrow she felt — her nature was to rebel, and though she could not show her rebellion openly, due to her strict up-bringing and the authoritarian ways of her father, it simmered in her breast with an ever-increasing desire for power. Power, to her, was the ultimate weapon. She craved power to be able to turn her back on "Them" and to take her revenge for all the neglect and abandonment that life had brought her so far.

★ ★ ★

Unfortunately for Charlotte, however, her nature was a mass of contradictions, all due to her up-bringing. On the one hand, she felt inferior to others, but on the other, her father's infiltration of snobbishness made her also feel that she was superior, and gave her a sense of her own importance. This in turn was undermined, however, by her conviction, again gained from her up-bringing, that she was unloveable.

She undoubtedly felt herself to be unloveable in many ways. As she grew, she realized that she was always going to be a tiny person, and hated herself for not being tall. She ruined her eyes by copying out engravings, and had to wear spectacles, which added to her conviction that she was plain. In later years, her publisher, George Smith of Smith, Elder, confirmed that indeed, Charlotte was correct in believing herself to be plain.

He described her as "interesting rather than attractive. She was very small, and had a quaint, old-fashioned look. Her head seemed too large for her body. She had fine eyes, but her face was marred by the shape of the mouth and by the complexion. There was but little feminine charm about her; and of this fact she herself was uneasily and perpetually conscious. It may seem strange that the possession of genius did not lift her above the weakness of an excessive anxiety about her personal appearance. But I believe she would have given all her genius and her fame to have been beautiful. Perhaps few women ever existed more anxious to be pretty than she, or more angrily conscious of the circumstance that she was *not* pretty."

★ ★ ★

We have already seen that any individual's basic motivation in life is the regard and approval of others, and that the self sees itself as it is reflected by the attitudes of others. Charlotte saw herself as inferior and unloveable, and when she declared that she had resigned herself to being an old maid, she was denying the thing she wanted most in life — love. Her psychological reflexes had persuaded her that she did not want to marry in order to defend herself against rejection, simply because she was convinced that no-one would want to marry her.

But the question of marriage, was to come later. Even in the five years that the children lived quietly at the Parsonage after the deaths of Maria and Elizabeth, Charlotte was struggling to come to terms with the conflicts in her personality which brought on insecurity and anxiety and guilt feelings. In her day and age, a woman was highly regarded if she was beautiful, and Charlotte knew she was not, and never would be. Well then, argued her unconscious, she would seek power instead — the power of the mind and of intellect. When — some remote day in the future — she was very powerful, then she would not feel inferior, and somehow, she would find that everyone treated her differently.

Charlotte was a fighter. She was rebellious and aggressive, though her self-control rarely allowed her to display these qualities, and she often gave way to distress and despair because of her neurotic personality. But all her life, she fought to establish herself as an individual, in spite of the psychological difficulties that made this an almost impossible task.

During these five years, the Group and the fantasy world of Glasstown brought her tremendous solace and relief. In the fantasy world, she was one of four all-powerful beings — the Genii — who could sway men's destinies and not only kill people but bring them back to life again. She could consciously win the approval of her Papa and Aunt with her demure and quiet manners, and despise society and the shallowness of material desires as she had been taught as a child, but in Angria, the kingdom that developed out of Glasstown, her unconscious could indulge itself in material delights, silken curtains, beautiful gowns, gorgeous settings, as much as she wished. Later, as she entered her teens and her sexual feelings began to waken, she could consciously repress them, but could write of virile heroes and immoral sexual encounters that would have made her blush for shame if she had applied them to herself.

This applied to all the children except Anne. They would never forget the stern moral code and sense of duty instilled into them by their Aunt, and on the surface they were all well-behaved, well-mannered and extremely moral. But in the worlds of fantasy deeply hidden, amoral emotions could be freely called forth, men could indulge in affairs with their mistresses, they could get drunk, swear and behave in any sort of wild licencious fashion their creators chose.

Charlotte's early hero in Glasstown was the Duke of Wellington, of whose daring exploits she had read in the newspapers, Later, however, she moved on to the amorous adventures of his son in the story, Arthur Augustus Adrian Wellesley, Marquis of Douro and Duke of Zamorna, Emperor of Angria. She chose to write about him through the eyes of another figure, Lord Charles Wellesley, and when I discussed with a psychiatrist the fact that she had taken a man for her central character and not a woman — which surely would have been more natural, as she could have then identified herself with her beautiful woman heroine — the psychiatrist gave me this reply:

"She chose a man so that she could have the best of both worlds. In him, since men were dominant in her society, she could be in control, and yet have a wide variety of experiences with women."

It is a significant fact, which bears comparison with Charlotte's male hero, that both "Moll Flanders" and "Fanny Hill" were written by men.

★ ★ ★

In 1830, Patrick, still concerned with his children's education, once again decided to send his eldest daughter, at least, to school, and in an effort to raise the necessary funds, consulted Miss Elizabeth Firth, the family's old friend, who was now a married woman. She conferred with Charlotte's god-parents, the Reverend and Mrs Atkinson, who were also old family friends from the Thornton days, and the childless couple expressed themselves as only too happy to assist with the education of their god-daughter. But Patrick did not want to make the same mistake as at Cowan Bridge, and the school chosen for

Charlotte to attend was the Misses Woolers' academy for young ladies at Roe Head, near Dewsbury, which was new, very select and highly recommended.

So, in January 1831, Charlotte, who was almost fifteen, was sent away once again to school. It was a terrible blow to the Group, who were now deeply engrossed in their fantasy world, and Charlotte trembled at the thought of mixing with strangers. But she had recognized that education was a means to power, and was growing up. The fantasy world had served its purpose, she decided, and the four children held a solemn conclave to end the kingdom of Glasstown. A farewell speech was made. Glasstown would be no more, and Charlotte made a mighty effort to try and come to terms with the real world.

This, however, proved to be more difficult than she had imagined, although the school was a friendly, kindly organized institution, very different to Cowan Bridge. Charlotte felt inferior and out of place amongst the other "young ladies", and on her first day, hid herself behind the schoolroom curtains where she could cry, as she thought, in private. But she was discovered by another newcomer to the school, Ellen Nussey, and this meeting led to a friendship that was to last until the end of Charlotte's life.

Charlotte made two friends while at Roe Head, Ellen and another girl called Mary Taylor, and her choice of these two particular girls is an interesting one, considering her own personality, for they were almost like two reflections of the two sides of her own nature. Ellen was a dainty, well-brought-up young lady — Margaret Lane describes her as seeming always to be "a gentle, charming person, conventional, pious, unintellectual, faithful, discreet — the perfect confidante for stormier, stronger natures." The sort of young lady, in fact, that Papa would have wished his daughter to become (except that he valued intellect).

Mary Taylor, on the other hand, represented Charlotte's inward personality of rage and rebellion, and, unlike Charlotte, she had not been repressed in childhood, but spoke her mind. She was, says Margaret Lane, "a natural rebel. She was outspoken where Ellen was tactful, original where Ellen was conventional, and revolutionary in matters in which Ellen and Charlotte would stand together against change." In other words, she was the inner Charlotte which hid behind the quiet, repressed exterior — she was what Charlotte would like to have been if she had dared.

The question arises of whether Charlotte loved her two friends, for as we have seen, she was hostile and suspicious of love. But perhaps Robert Keefe can shed some light on the situation. In CHARLOTTE BRONTË'S WORLD OF DEATH he expresses the opinion that she carried all through her life the need to "idolize and adore" people who captured her imagination, but that she probably did not feel that her adoration could ever be reciprocated. We shall see later that, if she *did* love, she gave an embarrassingly unreserved devotion to the loved one, but also, remained convinced that she herself was unloveable. How then can we explain her feelings towards Ellen and Mary?

Robert Keefe suggests that she

unconsciously adopted what he describes as "the classic pose of the novelist — voyeurism", and that she considered herself merely an onlooker, who stood aside and watched the affections of others being given and received, but never expected or thought herself worthy of love.

There is a good deal of truth in this, for although Charlotte made various attempts to live "in the real world", she often showed symptoms of stress brought on by conflict between the real and the fantasy when forced to face reality. Thus we see that there were many occasions when she showed some of the symptoms of stressful behaviour, such as severe headaches, irritability, self-hatred, a feeling of ugliness, repressed anger, misery, and a dread of the future, as well as collapse into nervous illness.

There are also signs that she did regard herself to some extent as an "onlooker", as she wrote in a letter to Ellen when both had left school:

"I have two studies, you are my study for the success, the credit, and the respectability of a quiet, tranquil character; Mary is my study for the contempt, the remorse, the misconstruction which follows the development of feelings in themselves noble, warm, generous, devoted and profound, but which, being too fully revealed, too frankly bestowed, are not estimated at their real value. I never hope to see in this world a creature more truly noble. She would die willingly for one she loved. Her intellect and attainments are of the very highest standard."

This letter is also revealing of Charlotte's own passion of deep feeling, which she felt she would never be able to show or give freely, lest it should be misunderstood — the result of her repression and neurosis. Instead of declaring herself, she gives all the credit for her own stored-up warmth of heart and achievements to her friend Mary, her "other self".

★ ★ ★

Although the Group had held a meeting to destroy Angria and Glasstown, Charlotte found that she could not live without it, and while she was at Roe Head, she and Branwell continued their saga by letter, including the various characters at school as figures in their stories. Emily had by this time broken away to a kingdom of her own — Gondal — which she shared with Anne. But Charlotte and Branwell were closer than ever mentally, strained together by the fantasy without which neither could exist. Branwell even tramped the long journey over the moors — some twenty miles — to visit his sister, and they spent an ecstatic day together. And when Charlotte returned home in the middle of 1832, their Angrian fantasy flourished as deeply as ever.

On her last day at school, Charlotte made one pitiful attempt to try and pull her fantasy and the real world together. She had worked extremely hard at her lessons — after all, knowledge was power — but on her final day she said to Ellen:

"I should for once like to feel *out and out* a schoolgirl; I wish something would happen! Let us run round the fruit garden; perhaps we shall meet someone, or we may have a fine for trespass."

And so they did. But of course, this was the real world, and nothing did happen. Charlotte was not surprised. She had not really expected that it would. It was only in Angria that things happened to her, and she was glad, though she had been reasonably happy at Roe Head, to return home to the forbidden fruit of erotic fantasy once more.

(ii)

Charlotte returned to Haworth with a new poise. She had been out into "exile", which was what they all considered separation from the Parsonage to be whenever they ventured into the world outside, and she had survived the ordeal, won intellectual honours and made two friends. She took over command and leadership of the Group, and the next few years were spent at home quietly, teaching her sisters all that she had learned while at school.

Yet her inferiority and the neurotic side of her personality were still there, unresolved, and as much in conflict with the powerful part of her character as ever. For instance, although she and her school friends had (as school-girls will) vowed to keep in touch, Charlotte, with her fear that she was unloveable, was pleased and surprised to find that Ellen kept her promise and wrote faithfully to her "dear C.".

Even Mrs Gaskell comments on what we know to be Charlotte's neurotic fear that she would be rejected, and wrote that she was "struck afresh by the absence of hope, which formed such a strong characteristic in Charlotte . . . In after-life, I was painfully impressed with the fact, that Miss Brontë never dared to allow herself to look forward with hope; that she had no confidence in the future . . . "

In any relationship outside the Group, Charlotte was timid and vulnerable. Mrs Gaskell wrote that she was "always fearful of loving too much; of wearying the objects of her affection; and thus she was often trying to restrain her warm feelings, and was ever chary of that presence so invariably welcome to her true friends."

Ellen, however, remained steadfast in

her correspondence, and Charlotte gained a great deal of pleasure from her letters, and those of Mary. She told Ellen of her daily round, painting a picture of quiet, leisurely days with her sisters, and the occasional social event — "We are expecting company this afternoon, and on Tuesday next we shall have all the female teachers of the Sunday-school to tea."

What Ellen and Mary never knew, however, was that beneath the decorum of Parsonage life, the fantasy world of Angria burned with as strong a flame as ever, and in fact, the year 1833, when Charlotte celebrated her seventeenth birthday, was very possibly the year when she produced more literary work than before or after in her life.

At seventeen, Charlotte was growing up, and all the sexual desires and strivings of a passionate nature were developing more fully than ever beneath a demure exterior. But at this point in her life, there was no possibility of Charlotte bestowing her build-up of passion on a man. She met very few men, and apart from her father and brother, she considered them an alien species.

Besides, she had her romantic hero, Arthur Augustus Adrian Wellesley, Marquis of Douro and Duke of Zamorna, Emperor of Angria, to satisfy her cravings, and apart from a few small overflows of excessive emotion into some of her letters to Ellen (harmless enough, and *not* a sign that Charlotte was a lesbian, nor that her feelings towards Ellen were anything other than warmly affectionate) Charlotte let her passions loose in her writing about Zamorna's amoral activities.

Her ideal lover was masterful, virile, cruel and fatally attractive to women. We have already noted that Charlotte felt the need to "idolize and adore", and she could not help patterning her idol to some extent on her father, and searching in her ideal love for the father she had never possessed emotionally. And so, Zamorna was magnificently dominating. Margot Peters comments that "she could not separate sexuality from domination since she could not free herself from the powerful authority of her father."

When it came to men or love, it was not likely that the seventeen-year-old Charlotte would ever consider an "ordinary" man in the real world to measure up in any way to her ideal. The clergymen who visited at Haworth, the village lads, would all have seemed equally lacking and insipid when compared to Zamorna's magnetic charm. So we can see that Charlotte was ill-equipped to enter into a love relationship with anyone at all of the opposite sex. Any human man, to her, would have fallen woefully short of her imaginary hero.

Yet though she idealized a figure who would have been irresistible to any woman, and could have taken his pick of beautiful, rich and charming heroines, in the unlikely event that such a person should ever have come her way, in real life, he would not have looked twice at the tiny, neurotic girl. For, once removed from the confines of home and the Group, Charlotte was a pathetic figure, crippled by her conflicts and her feelings of inferiority.

We can deduce therefore that such was the influence of the Group that it out-weighed Charlotte's personality and her sense of individuality, and she had not managed to achieve any confidence in herself when removed from the Group environment and placed in another situation. She thought people would not like her, so she behaved in either a withdrawn or an aggressive manner in order to protect herself from rejection.

She herself was aware of these two sides of her nature to some extent, although she did not realize that it was the protection and security of the Group which made her a different person at home to the awkward and prickly personality she assumed when out in the world.

To Ellen, she wrote, concerning her first proposal, which came from Ellen's brother, Henry Nussey, whom she had rejected:

"I was aware that Henry knew so little of me he could hardly be conscious to whom he was writing. Why, it would startle him to see me in my natural home character; he would think I was a wild, romantic enthusiast indeed. I could not sit all day long making a grave face before my husband. I would laugh, and satirise, and say whatever came into my head first. And if he were a clever man, and loved me, the whole world weighed in the balance against his smallest wish should be light as air."

Again, she gave away the fact that she was unable to enter into a natural, loving relationship with a man, and that unconsciously she must "idolize and adore" by telling Ellen: "I had not, and could not have that intense attachment which would make me willing to die for him; and, if ever I marry, it must be in that light of adoration that I will regard my husband."

Later, she was to comment in another letter to Ellen: "At home, you know, I talk with ease, and am never shy — never weighed down and oppressed by that miserable *mauvais honte* which torments and constrains me elsewhere."

But her gaiety and spontaneity were crushed and concealed by her constant inferiority feelings when away from home, and she was always haunted by the spectre of possible rejection. We do not, unfortunately, have a record of her dreams, which would probably give us an indication of how deeply her unconscious feared she was unloveable, but it is worth mentioning that one particular dream was recorded, and was described in later years to Mrs Gaskell by Mary Taylor, to whom Charlotte had confided it when they were both school-girls.

Mary recalled that: "She used to speak of her two elder sisters, Maria and Elizabeth, who died at Cowan Bridge. I used to believe them to have been wonders of talent and kindness. She told me, early one morning, that she had just been dreaming; she had been told that she was wanted in the drawing-room, and it was Maria and Elizabeth. I was eager for her to go on, and when she said there was no more, I said, 'but go on! *Make it out! I know you can.*' She said she would not; she wished she had not dreamed, for it did not go on nicely; they were changed; they had forgotten what they used to care for. They were very fashionably dressed, and began criticising the room, etc."

So here, we have a glimpse of how Charlotte's unconscious feared rejection even from her own dear, dead sisters. How much more must she have feared to be rejected by the living people whom she met outside the Parsonage walls.

A few months after leaving school, she accepted an invitation to visit Ellen's home, and Ellen recollected later how she and Charlotte "crept away together from household life as much as we could. Charlotte liked to pace the plantations or seek seclusion in the fruit garden; she was safe from visitors in these retreats. She was so painfully shy she could not bear any special notice. One day, on being led into dinner by a stranger, she trembled and nearly burst into tears."

In her later life, when she ventured out into the world as a governess, Charlotte's shyness gave way to defensive aggression, and the snobbery and superiority we have previously seen as inherited from her father often came into conflict with the necessity for servility and restraint (for a governess was, of course, regarded as practically a servant).

Charlotte was secretly contemptuous of her employers, whom she regarded as uncultured and intellectually inferior to herself — though they were rich and she was poor — and she fumed inwardly against the fact that she had to accept a servile position and attitude in a household of strangers. She wrote bitter letters home, complaining about the way she was treated. Yet we can understand that she must have been a very difficult person to please, from the point of view of her employers.

Margaret Lane has recorded the other side of the coin, the reminiscences of a relation of Mrs Sidgwick of Stonegappe, with whom Charlotte spent a short period.

"She was, according to her own account, very unkindly treated," remembers a cousin of the family, "but it is clear that she had no gifts for the management of children, and was also in a very morbid condition the whole time. My cousin Benson Sidgwick, now vicar of Ashby Parva, certainly on one occasion threw a Bible at Miss Brontë! and all that another cousin can recollect of her is that if she was invited to walk to church with them, she thought she was being ordered about like a slave; if she was not invited, she imagined she was excluded from the family circle."

In addition to the fact that she was temperamentally unsuited for the life of a governess, that her neuroticism made her over-react to all the little daily incidents that befell her, and that she had no idea of how to cope with normal children, Charlotte had an extra obstacle to overcome which we have previously mentioned: she was still in the grip of her fantasy world of Angria, and was frustrated because so much of her time was taken up with her duties that she was unable to escape into her imaginary land, and the consolation of writing and thinking about her beloved Zamorna.

In her first situation as a teacher at Roe Head, the school where she had previously been a pupil, she suffered many of the symptoms of stress which we have already noted when reality comes into conflict with fantasy. The "stress factor" for Charlotte followed a pattern that is outlined in THE HEALTH & FITNESS HANDBOOK.

First of all, the body prepares to either fight the stress or run away from it, and if the problem cannot be resolved physically, then the second — adaptation — stage takes place, leading to such symptoms as hypertension, aches, pains and severe headaches, constant irritability, lack of interest in life in general, morbidity, and in Charlotte's case, extreme melancholia. This is followed, if no action is taken, by complete collapse into illness either physical or mental.

We know that Charlotte struggled heroically, comforted only by her imaginative dreams of Angria, which took on a deeply erotic tone, and that she at last managed to take action to break her decline into collapse when, anxious about the health of Anne, who was at this time a pupil at the school, she staged a scene with the headmistress, Miss Wooler, when probably all her pent-up rage and frustration came seething to the surface. The result was that both Anne and Charlotte returned to the Parsonage; but the kindly Miss Wooler, though deeply shaken by Charlotte's uncharacteristic outburst, persuaded her to return and carry on teaching.

Charlotte had had duty instilled into

her by Aunt as a young girl, and, feeling it her duty to return, she did so, but she became caught up once again in all the symptoms of extreme stress, and, so Mary Taylor recalled: "From that time her imaginations became gloomy or frightful; she could not help it, not help thinking. She could not forget the gloom, could not sleep at night nor attend in the day."

In fact, she was saved from a complete collapse only because Miss Wooler persuaded her to see a doctor, and he at once prescribed a return home, saying that if she did not go back to the Parsonage, she would very possibly lose either her reason or her life. Once back in the security of the Group, with the stress of trying to cope with a reality beyond her capabilities removed, Charlotte quickly recovered both her health and spirits.

★ ★ ★

It is to Charlotte's credit that, in spite of her many psychological problems, she managed to mature enough to recognize that, if she ever wanted to become a published writer — a person of influence, of power — she would never do so by remaining within the realms of Angria, and at the age of twenty-three, when she was at home in between her two spells of being a private governess, she wrote a reluctant farewell to the fantasy behind which she had hidden from reality for over ten years.

"I have now written a great many books and for a long time have dwelt on the same characters and scenes and subjects . . . my readers have been habituated to one set of features . . . but we must change, for the eye is tired of the picture so oft recurring and now so familiar.

" . . . it is no easy theme to dismiss from my imagination the images which have filled it so long; they were my friends and my intimate acquaintances, and I could with little labour describe to you the faces, the voices, the actions, of those who peopled my thoughts by day, and not seldom stole strangely even into my dreams by night. When I depart from these I feel almost as if I stood on the threshold of a home, and were bidding farewell to its inmates . . . "

But Charlotte had recognised that her tales of Angria were self-indulgent (not to mention shocking!) and that if she wanted to succeed as a writer in the real world, she must write something more to the public taste. And by now, after trying to earn a living as a teacher and governess, all her mind was set on somehow becoming a published writer.

As we know, she had long ago decided that intellect was power, and that if she were a writer, it would not matter that she was small and plain and insignificant. The public would know her only through her writing. So she determined that what she wrote in the future should be aimed at possible publication.

And it was she, the fighter, the rebel, who in spite of her neurotic drawbacks of character, led and encouraged the other members of the Group to keep on and on battering against the walls of publishing houses until at long last, she achieved her great ambition and broke down those high walls, grim and forbidding, with something that had come from her pen — in her case, it was to be JANE EYRE which, after a long and wearisome effort, brought her the power she had longed for all her life.

This book is about the Brontë's search for love. We have already seen that Charlotte consciously renounced any dreams of ever finding love in real life, in favour of a search for power. Yet in spite of her fears that no-one would want her, she received no less than four proposals during her life, and was, in fact, the only one of the girls to marry. Two of the proposals we can dismiss, as Charlotte wisely did, for the gentlemen concerned were not in love with her, and she did not love them. And, to her romantic soul, love and adoration meant everything.

Her first proposal, when she was twenty-three, came from Ellen's brother, Henry Nussey, who was then a curate, and required a wife for purely practical purposes to assist him with his work. He therefore made a business-like list of suitable young ladies he might approach, and proceeded to write to each in turn. Charlotte, significantly, was not even at the top of the list. He only wrote to her when his first choice of a suitable wife turned him down.

Charlotte, of course, did not know this, but, tempting though the prospect was of achieving the status of a married woman, she knew she could not accept. We have already heard some of her comments to Ellen on the subject of Henry's proposal, and to him she replied almost immediately, telling him that:

"You are aware that I have many reasons to feel grateful to your family, and I have peculiar reasons for affection towards one at least of your sisters, and also that I highly esteem yourself — do not therefore accuse me of wrong motives when I say that my answer to your proposal must be a *decided negative*."

She knew she might never come across a Zamorna in real life, but even so, she shrank from marriage to the priggish Henry. The position of wife to an insignificant clergyman clashed with her desire for power — besides, she cared nothing for Henry himself — and she was sensible enough to realize that she would have been stifled, frustrated, and put under stress with which she would have been unable to cope, had she accepted him.

It is also possible that beneath the conscious reasons she gave for refusing him — the fact that she did not think she was the sort of person he wanted, and that she would not have made him happy — her neurotic personality panicked at the thought of trying to come to terms with real-life marriage, and she shied away from the idea of such an intimate relationship with a man, frightened by all it would involve. She longed for love, yet her personality was unable to deal with all that went with it.

Her second proposal came a short time later, and Charlotte, again having refused the gentleman concerned, decided to treat the whole matter as a joke in a letter to Ellen.

"I have an odd circumstance to relate to you, prepare for a hearty laugh," she wrote.

Apparently a young Irish curate who was visiting the Parsonage with his superior, commenced a lively flirtation with Charlotte, who, as we know, could be quite frivolous when in the company of the Group and behind the security of the Parsonage walls. The two men left after their visit, but a few days later, Charlotte received a proposal in the form of a passionate declaration of love from the young curate, Mr Price, whom she had met for only a few hours. She could not, of course, take him seriously.

"I hope you are laughing heartily," she wrote to Ellen. "This is not like one of my adventures, is it? . . . I am certainly doomed to be an old maid."

We can deduce from this that, although neither of the proposals she had so far received were acceptable to her, she was still convinced — in spite of them — that she was unloveable, and could not imagine that there might be more to come in the future, possibly from men she could seriously consider as husbands. Yet she had never expected to be proposed to at all, and already two members of the opposite sex had declared their interest in her. Her conviction that she would never be wanted remained basically unshaken, and she continued to feel wary and hostile in her attitude to men.

★ ★ ★

These two proposals came when she was comparatively young. The other two occured much later in her life, and in between, an event took place which brought her fantasies into conflict with the real world, made her dreams realities, and broke down all her barriers of reserve so that she metaphorically fell at the feet of the personification of her imaginary hero, and gave free rein to her need to "idolize and adore".

This was to be the most important emotional upheaval of her life, and in her neurotic passion and the unconscious expression of her inmost cravings for affection and a love she had never known, she was, as one might expect, bitterly hurt and unbearably wounded when, inevitably, her ardent devotion was rejected.

It took her two years to recover from the experience of a "love affair" which she did not even consciously recognize as having been a love affair at all, for the object of her affections was a married man, and Charlotte would have been horrified if, in her conscious mind, she had been aware of being sexually — or even emotionally — "in love" with someone else's husband.

The man in question was a foreigner. Charlotte met him when, in February of 1842, aged twenty-five, she and Emily went as pupils to the Pensionnat Heger, in Brussels, as part of a scheme to "brush up" and polish their languages and improve their cultural education before endeavouring to set up a school of their own — a project designed to avoid the governessing "in exile" and allow the girls to live and work together.

The proprietress of the school was a competent and efficient lady called Madame Heger, and it was her husband, Monsieur Constantin Heger, who took classes at the school, to whom Charlotte was irresistably drawn.

Margaret Lane describes him as "a teacher of genius. He was of that ardent and dynamic temperament which insists on an emotional *rapport* between master and pupil; he felt obliged to dominate and control; or he could not teach, and he took an artist's pleasure in playing and extending his pupils intellectually through half-angry, half-loving demands on the emotions."

He was no Zamorna — Charlotte herself wrote of him in a letter to Ellen as "a little black ugly being, with a face that varies in expression. Sometimes he borrows the lineaments of an insane tom-cat, sometimes those of a delirious hyena; occasionally, but very seldom, he discards these perilous attractions and assumes an air not above 100 degrees removed from mild and gentlemanlike."

Yet he possessed all the characteristics that Charlotte, in her inmost heart, yearned for in a man. He was virile and very masculine; he was not too young, and was intellectual and sophisticated, with a sense of humour and a spell-binding charm; he was masterful and dominant; he could reduce her to tears, but when she wept, the sight of her weeping, as she put it "sets all things straight", for he was then all contrition.

And so Charlotte was inexplicably happy as a pupil — though whether she would have been as happy without the stimulating presence of M. Heger is a matter for doubt, for there were many things about life on the continent that she did not like. But in her unconscious, her world began to revolve around her teacher's presence, and her neurotic passion formed him into her god and her idol.

★ ★ ★

Events occurred which forced Charlotte and Emily to leave Brussels rather hurriedly. There had been illness at the Parsonage, and now Aunt Branwell was dying. The girls arrived at Haworth just too late for the funeral, to be confronted with the prospect of what further action they should take now.

Charlotte had been inwardly dismayed at having to part from her "Master", and when M. Heger, in a tactful and discreet letter to Mr Brontë, urged him to let at least one of the girls return to complete their studies, with the prospect of becoming a teacher at the school, she pleaded to be allowed to go, and it was eventually decided that she should return alone, while Emily stayed at home to supervise the day-to-day doings at the Parsonage.

So Charlotte went back to Brussels, unconscious of the fact that it was her feelings for M. Heger that were drawing her like a magnet, and thinking consciously only of the benefits of further study. But by this time, Madame had become aware of the English girl's emotional fervour towards her husband, and determined to put a stop to it. So on Charlotte's return, the girl found, to her dismay, that everything was different. Promoted to teacher, she discovered that she hardly ever saw M. Heger, and rarely alone. Madame was always discouragingly present in the background, and her attitude towards Charlotte, which had formerly been approving and friendly, had changed to a distinct coolness.

The girl could not bear to be so close to, and yet so far from, her idol, unable to express her feelings, and she became more and more unhappy. Eventually, after struggling for a long while to cope with her loneliness and the stress of repressing her unconscious neurotic passions, she gave in her notice, and returned to England. She described her last few days in Brussels to Ellen.

"I suffered much before I left Brussels. I think, however long I live, I shall not forget what the parting with M. Heger cost me; it grieved me so much to grieve him, who has been so true, kind and disinterested a friend."

★ ★ ★

Once back at the Parsonage, however, Charlotte's neuroticism drove her into writing letter after letter to her "Master". They were not love letters in the conventional sense, and he replied openly to them at first. But with her separation from him, Charlotte had now realized — although the word "love" was never mentioned — that she could not live without some contact, some approving word from her idol. Unconsciously she had opened the flood-gates of passions that had been sternly repressed; she had transferred her longing fantasy for Zamorna to a living and breathing man, she was enmeshed in her need to "idolize and adore".

220

M. Heger recognized the tone her letters took on, and became alarmed at her intensity. His replies became infrequent, and he asked her not to write to him more than twice a year. But to Charlotte, he was now an obsession. She could not help herself, and her yearning broke through in unrestrained and embarrassing revelations of now she was suffering from his withdrawal and his refusal to answer the letters she *had* to write.

"Once more goodbye, Monsieur; it hurts to say good-bye even in a letter. Oh, it is certain that I shall see you again one day — it must be so — for as soon as I have earned enough money to go to Brussels I shall go there — I shall see you again if only for a moment . . . "

And then: "For six months I have been awaiting a letter from Monsieur — six months waiting is very long, you know. However, I do not complain, and I shall be richly rewarded for a little sorrow if you will now write . . . "

Then, when still he did not reply, Charlotte's words became more frenzied and abandoned.

"Day and night I find neither rest nor peace. If I sleep I am disturbed by tormenting dreams" (those dreams of rejection again!) "in which I see you, always severe, always grave, always incensed against me . . . All I know is that I cannot, that I will not, resign myself to lose wholly the friendship of my master . . . If my master withdraws his friendship from me entirely I shall be altogether without hope; if he gives me a little — just a little — I shall be satisfied — happy; I shall have a reason for living on, for working.

"Monsieur, the poor have not need of much to sustain them — they ask only for the crumbs that fall from the rich man's table. But if they are refused the crumbs they die of hunger . . . "

Yet still there was no word from M. Heger, and Charlotte struggled on through a miasma of melancholy and rejection, writing anguished poetry to try and ease the ache in her heart. She sent one last, pitiful letter after the prescribed six months in which she had firmly not written him a line.

" . . . To forbid me to write to you,

to refuse to answer me would be to tear from me my only joy on earth, to deprive me of my last priviledge — a priviledge I shall never consent willingly to surrender . . . "

She begged, she pleaded, she besought him earnestly to write and give her some sort of peace. It was fortunate she did not know that on reading this desperate plea from a tormented heart, M. Heger tore it up and threw it into his waste-paper basket, as in fact, he had done with the others.

It was Madame, his wife, who secretly retrieved them, pieced and stitched them together, and kept them — for what purpose we do not exactly know — so that some at least of them are still in existence today.

M. Heger never wrote to Charlotte again. He was not an unkind man, but he recognized the fact that her devotion was neurotic, that she wanted him to let her "idolize and adore", and he was not prepared to accept any further involvement with her. But it took Charlotte, as we have already heard, at least two years of utter misery to come to terms with his rejection of her, and turn her mind, as she had done in the past when unable to confront physical or spiritual rejection, to renew her dreams of finding power through her writing.

It is doubtful whether, even in her wildest dreams, Charlotte ever envisaged a full-scale *affaire* with M. Heger. Indeed, as she herself wrote to him: "I should not know what to do with a friendship entire and complete — I am not used to it."

What she really longed for was not sexual gratification but simply his touch, not as a lover but as a companion; the feeling of strong masculine arms about her (as a substitute for her father's arms, in fact). What she wanted was the "stroking" she had never received as a child.

And yet, of course, she was not a child any longer, so sexual desires must have played an unconscious part in her passion for him, although as far as physical sex went, she was completely innocent, and had no conscious knowledge of what it involved. Passion and sensuality she had experienced in her Angrian dreams, but practical sex between a man and a woman was something of which she was ignorant, and which would probably have frightened and disgusted her if her "Master" had mistaken her adoration for lust, and tried to seduce her.

★ ★ ★

Later, when she had achieved the fame and power she sought, and her best-seller JANE EYRE had swept England, Charlotte began to live a different sort of life to her "governessing", and was introduced into society as a celebrity by her publisher, George Smith, of Smith, Elder. There have been various speculations as to whether there was ever any suggestion of a romance between the tiny, quaint little woman and the dashing young publisher, but, on George Smith's part at least, this is unlikely. He valued her as an author, and recognized her genius, but he found Charlotte, as we have previously heard, distinctly not the sort of creature to turn his head. She, in her turn, probably felt very much attracted to the handsome Smith, but, with the warning of M. Heger behind her, she firmly refused to give way to her feelings, and sternly repressed any temptation to let herself fall "in love" again.

However, a third partner in the publishing firm, James Taylor, felt very differently, and in 1849, when Charlotte had just completed the manuscript of another novel, SHIRLEY, Mr Taylor, who was travelling in the north, offered to come and collect it in person to take it to London.

He duly arrived at the Parsonage, and Charlotte found him to be completely uncongenial to her. She did not like his appearance — he was not very tall, blunt and ungentlemanly in his ways, and had red hair. Nevertheless, she received him politely, and handed over the manuscript. After a day at the Parsonage, he left, and Charlotte thought no more about him.

But he thought a great deal about her, and later that year, when she went to London at George Smith's invitation, Mr Taylor was again in evidence. Charlotte wrote to Ellen:

"Mr Taylor — the little man — has again shown his parts, in fact I suspect he is of the Helstone order of men" (a reference to a character in SHIRLEY) " — rigid, despotic and self-willed. He tries to be very kind and even to express sympathy sometimes, but he does not manage it. He has a determined, dreadful nose in the middle of his face which when poked into my countenance cuts into my soul like iron. Still he is horribly intelligent, quick, searching, sagacious, and with a memory of relentless tenacity . . . "

Unfortunately for Charlotte, James Taylor had fallen in love with her, and it was from him that her third proposal of marriage came, first by means of a courtship through letters after she had returned to Haworth, and then, just before her thirty-fifth birthday, with a personal visit. Charlotte's feelings for him were mixed. When they were apart, she could reflect that it was touching to be wanted, to be loved, to be needed — but whenever she was near him, she found his physical presence so unattractive that it was difficult even to be polite. She could not bring herself to accept his proposal, and he departed for ever out of her life.

So once again, Charlotte resigned herself to spinsterhood. She was no longer young, and she recognized drearily that she would always be plain. But she had the literary world at her feet; she had met many celebrities and writers she had previously admired from afar, she was lionized and sought after. This, she felt, would be the pattern of her life in the future. But one more man was to love her — and this time, she was to marry him.

Reality finally claimed Charlotte in the person of her husband. He was not rich, not cruel and masterfully arrogant, not particularly handsome. No-one could have been further from the lover of her early dreams. The man in question was none other than her father's curate, Arthur Bell Nicholls, who had been a familiar figure to Charlotte at the Parsonage for several years, and for whom she had barely spared a glance.

He began by acting strangely when in her presence, and then, one December evening, he blurted out a passionate declaration of love for her in a manner which shook her, as she reported to Ellen, with "a strange shock". She did not know what to say, and told him she would give him an answer the next day.

Charlotte did not love Mr Nicholls, but she was moved to pity by the obvious depth of his feeling, the fact that he loved her for herself alone, not because she was famous, and because she recognized that he too feared rejection — just as she had feared rejection so many times herself in the past. In addition, her father, who was becoming a tyrant in his old age, was furious when he heard about the proposal, and declared emphatically that he would never permit his daughter to marry a humble curate. He sternly forbade Charlotte to have anything more to do with Mr Nicholls.

The eventual result of the tensions and passions aroused by Mr Nicholls's declaration of his feelings, the way in which her father had treated him, the fact that everyone in the household and the village thought it an unsuitable match, made Charlotte's reaction inevitable. She had always been rebellious.

After a long period of hesitancy, growing hatred of her father's tyranny over her and his forbidding her to lead a life of her own, a sense of her own loneliness (for the other three members of the Group were long since dead), secret letters and secret meetings, Charlotte allowed herself to be persuaded, in spite of the doubts and fears in her heart, to accept what real life had to offer, and marry Mr Nicholls. The wedding took place quietly at Haworth on Thursday, 29 June, 1854, when Charlotte was thirty-eight.

★ ★ ★

It seems, then, that Charlotte at least was successful in her search for love. She married; she became a wife to a man who was undoubtedly devoted to her. And yet, where was the fire, the joy, the passion, that she had so successfully imbued into Jane's love for Mr Rochester?

Before the wedding, Charlotte wrote to Ellen: "I am still very inexpectant. What I taste of happiness is of the soberest order. I trust to love my husband — I am grateful for his tender love to me. I believe him to be an affectionate, a conscientious, a high-principled man; and if, with all this, I should yield to regrets, that fine talents, congenial tastes and thoughts are not added, it seems to me I should be most presumptous and thankless."

No, she never found that quivering adoration which would have made her willing to die for her husband. It belonged only in Angria — and had withered away, leaving her disillusioned for ever when M. Heger rejected her. However, she was prepared to glean what happiness she could from her marriage, although from what we know of her brief period as a wife, there are ominous indications that it might not have proved to be entirely to Charlotte's liking once the first year, perhaps, was over.

Even Mrs Gaskell sensed that "I am sure that Miss Brontë could never have . . . been happy but with an exacting, rigid, law-giving, passionate man."

She began, however, to grow quite fond of her new husband in the weeks when she and Mr Nicholls were away on their honeymoon, visiting his family in Ireland. He became "my dear husband", and soon, "my dear Arthur" and "my dear boy". He even assumed some of the authority and possessiveness that Charlotte had so desired in the man she would eventually marry, and revealed an unexpected streak of sensitivity towards her moods and feelings.

But would Charlotte have grown to resent having her time to write disrupted, at being called upon whenever her husband required her presence for a walk on the moors, at not being her own mistress after so many years? Did she find sex a burden, or a pleasure? She does not reveal much to us, but hints at hesitancy in this direction in a letter to Ellen, written after six weeks of marriage.

"I know more of the realities of life than I once did. I think many false ideas are propagated perhaps unintentionally. I think those married women who indiscriminately urge their acquaintance to marry — much to blame. For my part — I can only say with deeper sincerity and fuller significance — what I always said in theory — Wait God's will. Indeed — indeed — Nell — it is a solemn and strange and perilous thing for a woman to become a wife. Man's lot is far — far different."

It is very likely that Charlotte would have found the demands her husband made upon her time and attention made her resentful, for after all, she was a writer and required time to write and contemplate. Moreover, she was a famous writer, and had a reputation to live up to, a public who claimed her work.

However, we shall never know how events might have developed, for Charlotte had not long left to live. Ever since her marriage, she had been plagued by annoying little illnesses like colds and sore throats — and it is significant here that neuroticism and stress often cause such physical symptoms. But early in the next year, 1855, she began to suffer from nausea and faintness, which were set down to the fact that she discovered she was pregnant.

It would pass, she was told, and then

she would have the baby to look forward to. But it did not pass. Charlotte began vomiting, and could not eat. She grew rapidly worse, and it was during this time, on a sickbed of great pain, that she managed to pencil a note to Ellen, which assured her friend that: " . . . I find my husband the tenderest nurse, the kindest support, the best earthly comfort that ever woman had. His patience never fails . . . "

Late in March, when she was obviously dying, she roused to hear her husband praying God would spare her, and whispered:

"Oh, I am not going to die, am I? He will not separate us, we have been so happy."

So even in her last words, she was unable to reconcile the real and the fantasy. Her brief life with Mr Nicholls had been content in its way, but far from ecstatic. Yet the cry in her heart came straight from Angria.

On 31 March, 1855, she and her unborn child passed for ever from this earth, leaving a grief-stricken husband and a father who had outlived all his strange and gifted children alone to mourn.

★ ★ ★

It is generally believed that her death was caused by consumption, but Philip Rhodes has a different theory, and writes: "It is quite clear that she died of hyperenesis gravidarum, the pernicious vomiting of pregnancy", adding: "The disorder only seems to become excessive in those who display neuroticism." He is certain, therefore, that Charlotte's neurosis was "the ultimate cause of her death", and that the disease may also have been an unconscious rejection of the baby she was carrying.

So far as the baby was concerned, Charlotte almost certainly did not want it. She did not like children, she was not the stuff of which mothers are made, and she showed little or no concern or pleasure about being pregnant. Indeed, she was probably utterly dismayed at her condition, so Philip Rhodes is probably right in concluding that unconsciously, she rejected it.

In her last few months, reality proved too strong for her fragile hold upon it, and she was unable once again to cope with the stress engendered by the conflict between her real situation and the world of her imagination — in other words, her books.

It is worth noting, in conclusion, that of the four great novels she left to posterity, two of them, VILLETTE and THE PROFESSOR, were based on the story of her love for M. Heger, which must have haunted her all her life; and JANE EYRE was a passionate declaration of herself as an individual, as well as a deeply gripping love story. SHIRLEY was a study of her enigmatic sister Emily, as she might have been if born into different circumstances.

The scope of her work was not wide, but she knew the anguish of loving and being rejected, and she knew Emily in the way that she knew all the other members of the Group. She also knew the pain of being herself, small, plain and insignificant, and it was her very familiarity with her subjects, and the suppressed passions and deeply felt emotions she poured into her work, that gave her books their immediacy and vitality and power to grip the reader. The rest we must attribute quite simply to that mysterious ingredient called genius.

Part Four

Emily

Emily

(i)

AT first sight, Emily Brontë appears to have been the most self-sufficient and independent of all the children. She does not, like Charlotte and Anne, seem to have sought love. She had no friends; and indeed she gives one the impression when looking at her life in retrospect, that had anyone tried to gain her affection, she would have responded with either amusement or scorn, depending on her mood.

But a closer examination will show that Emily possibly suffered far more than any of the other children from emotional deprivation in her early years. Charlotte, as we have seen, became neurotic, but Emily lived out her whole life with a personality completely undermined and crippled by lack of love when she was only a small girl. The others coped with the traumas they suffered as best they could — Emily was to be so crushed that she was unable to attempt to cope, and her emotional and mental capabilities were unequal to the task of overcoming the events that occurred in her very early years.

We have no evidence as to how her birth, in 1818, was received by her parents. But her mother, exhausted after bearing five infants in such a short space of time, could probably spare only a token affection for her new baby, and was glad to leave the child in the care of Nancy and Sarah. The year before, Patrick had been presented with a boy — a son at last — to carry on the family name, and it is all too likely that, now that he had his son, he would not have been very interested in the birth of yet another girl.

He already had three, as well as his beloved boy. If it had been a second son, now, that might have been different, but what was a fourth girl to him? We can be reasonably certain that, after a perfunctory enquiry as to whether all was well, Patrick put thoughts of the new baby out of his mind, regarding it as just another mouth to feed.

So from the first, Emily had little or no contact with her father, but it is likely that she did grow to have a happy relationship with her mother. We know that she was a pretty child, and her mother may have had a special affection for this latest addition to her family. However, when she was approaching her second birthday, two traumatic events occurred in Emily's small world. Another sister, Anne, was born; and the family moved to Haworth.

I do not think that the advent of Anne put an end to Emily's closeness to her Mama. They were both the "babies of the family", and Emily would have enjoyed helping her mother to care for the tiny new creature that had entered the house. She was not of a jealous nature, and was quite used to being one of a number of children. Perhaps, to her, Anne was like a doll, and she delighted in her small sister.

But the move to Haworth was different. Just as the two-year-old was coming to terms with her surroundings, those surroundings changed drastically, and she was plunged into a new environment. The likelihood is that she would have clung all the closer to her mother, and that her Mama would have tried to respond to the toddler's unspoken plea for reassurance.

But it was at this point that the great tragedy of Emily's life occurred. Within months, her mother had become ill with her last, fatal illness, and was confined to the sick-room, out of Emily's reach. Probably the little girl never set eyes on her Mama again.

★ ★ ★

We have already seen that children respond to death in a different way to adults. When her mother eventually died, Emily, at three, would not have understood the difference between death and temporary separation. She only knew that her Mama was no longer there to touch, or to hold. Yet the death of her mother completely altered and stunted the little girl's personality.

In Sula Wolff's admirable CHILDREN UNDER STRESS, the author writes of the work of Dr Michael Rutter, whose examination of groups of bereaved children produced the conclusion that maternal death is especially related to possible psychiatric disturbance in the case of girls. Dr Rutter also puts forward a theory that the loss of a parent when the child is two or three is particularly damaging because it is at this time that the parent is most required by the child as a model for its identification of itself.

Another interesting point discovered by Dr Rutter was that, if bereavement *was* the cause of later emotional or psychiatric illness, the illness did not follow immediately on the bereavement. There was a gap of several years in most cases before any symptoms began to show themselves, and when a child had lost a parent at the age of about two to four, the illness did not make any marked appearance until puberty.

If we apply this to Emily, who lost her mother at the age of three, we will see that she appeared to show no symptoms of particular distress which manifested themselves to the people around her on the actual occasion of her mother's death — but in puberty, she did begin to emerge with a markedly different character to that of any ordinary young girl, and her behaviour as she grew older was accepted by the rest of the family as distinctly odd, although no-one seems to have queried the cause of it. They simply accepted her oddities and eccentricities as "just Emily".

But I do not think that Emily was born with any particularly perculiar quirks of character. Her oddities were caused by the great trauma of her mother's death — which, to the child, simply meant the disappearance of her mother from her surroundings — and the lack of contact with her father. The seeming coldness and absence of emotion in her personality, the transference of her affections to her pets and her home and the surrounding moors, her absolute dependence on the environment of the parsonage, were the direct result of a psychological "death" and period of mourning through which she passed when her Mama left her to fend for herself in a world which she could not face nor mature in.

Her emotional development, in fact, came to a standstill at the age of three, so far as contact with human beings was concerned — with one exception: her baby sister Anne, whom she had already learned to love. In later years, the apparently strong Emily was to cling to the apparently fragile Anne as her only prop in her dealings with the rest of humanity. She had no other guide to help her find her way through the maze of interpersonal relationships.

★ ★ ★

In early childhood, even a brief separation from the mother produces a pattern which can loosely be compared to "mourning", as though the mother is actually dead — and since her Mama did die, and never returned to her, Emily would have passed through these stages almost automatically. For while the elder children clung to Maria as a substitute mother, to Emily, the ties that bound her to her Mama were still very real, and Maria never took Mrs Brontë's place for her as she did for the other children.

First of all comes a stage of protest, when grief and anger are felt, and if

Emily cried a lot at the time her mother was ill, the others — if they noticed it at all — would have put it down to the fact that she was still "only a baby", or "just being a cry-baby".

Then the crying gives way to despair, and the child becomes apathetic, as grief is felt inwardly instead of outwardly. Here again, no-one would have noticed her reaction. Maria may have tried to comfort her young sister, but a child in this stage pays no attention and rejects any advances from anyone who is not the lost mother.

It is even possible that Aunt may have felt it her duty to console the bereaved Emily, but Aunt never made any impression at all upon Emily's personality, and the child made no attempt to adjust to a relationship with her mother's sister. Emily never paid any attention as she grew up to anything her Aunt said, as the other children did. She completely rejected her Aunt, her Aunt's religious creed and her Aunt's praise or admonitions.

The last step in the bereavement process is one of detachment. The child appears to return to normal, and to have forgotten the lost parent. But by now, the inner damage has been done, and in Emily's case, the result was that she had become so vulnerable to any further losses that she withdrew completely from any attempt to relate to other people in a loving and caring way — again with the exception of her sister Anne.

She refused, in fact, to face reality, which, as one psychologist has commented to me, is a symptom of severe parental deprivation, as seen in many cases of deprived children; and long before the Group and the fantasy worlds of Angria and Gondal were formed, Emily's unconscious was establishing a substitute — she simply did not develop emotionally at all, except in one direction. This did not happen at once however, but came gradually.

★ ★ ★

It has been remarked upon many times that when Emily was removed from the confines of the moors and the Parsonage, she became physically ill, but when, at the age of six, she was sent with the others to Cowan Bridge, there is no suggestion of her showing any symptoms of distress. But on the other hand, there is no suggestion either that she took any particular pleasure-from the petting and notice she received as the youngest girl in the school.

At this stage, her personality had not yet developed in the way it was to go at a later date. Emily was passive and uncaring. Even the deaths of Maria and Elizabeth seem to have made no impression on her — although this further loss may have been the trigger that launched her on her path to what she had become by the time she left home a second time, at the age of just seventeen, to accompany Charlotte to Roe Head, Miss Wooler's school, as a pupil. For between the years when she was six and when she was seventeen, all of them spent at home, Emily had developed a schizoid, or dual, personality.

★ ★ ★

She had lost her mother, and due to the "mourning" period, had been unable to accept anyone else in her mother's place. Therefore she had no model upon which to base her own identity. Yet an individual must form some sense of identity in order to survive, and in Emily's case, her personality had partially projected itself into her environment — the moors — which she felt were a part of herself.

She had also had to try and mature as the years passed and she grew older, and, having rejected the conventional methods of growth laid down by her Aunt, she had devised her own system of maturity.

Consequently, her primary personality, the tall, excessively shy girl the family knew, with her love of animals, her absolute devotion to the moors, her awkwardness in the presence of strangers, her reluctance to join in "ordinary" girlish activities, her need for freedom to wander her own familiar terrain and her periods of withdrawal into herself — this was a very much more mature person intellectually than all her contemporaries, for she had had to think deeply and ponder the depths of her conscious character in order to form the opinions she held. She was not interested in the opinions of others.

But in addition, the schizoid nature of her personality meant that she must always be with her "other self", the moors, and, later on, her fantasy world of Gondal, which resembled the wild Yorkshire countryside as much as Charlotte's Angria differed from what she had come to know as "reality". Emily's was a very complex and difficult personality to unravel, and that is why she has always seemed so much of an enigma to the casual observer.

★ ★ ★

We must not forget, either, that as Emily grew from six to seventeen, she was set apart by her own nature, but she was also a member of the Group. But as W. J. H. Sprott has pointed out in HUMAN GROUPS: "On occasion one may find a person quite completely indifferent to the attitudes of other members of a group, but of such a one we should most likely say that he was 'in' the group but not 'of' it. This, of course, is quite different from standing up against the group on occasion".

Again, he points out that "The pressure of the group on the individual is in the direction of conformity. It may be met with compliance or emotional rejection."

We have already seen that Emily's personality was such that she did not care either way about the approval of others, as most individuals do — she had her own ideas and her own standards — and so we can conclude that she went along with the Group, but emotionally rejected any part of it she did not need, at the same time joining enthusiastically in any part she *did* need: such as the creation of the fantasy worlds.

Emily and Anne appear to have had little say in matters of Glasstown and Angria, although the two older members of the Group generously included them in Glasstown activities when they wrote their stories. But at the age of thirteen, when Charlotte was away in Roe Head, Emily broke away to form her own fantasy world, into which she allowed only Anne.

Here we have another interesting point to consider. The primary personality of Emily — the girl who moved about the family home — was efficient, mature and assured in a quiet way, yet mannish and with definite opinions of her own. She had had no mother on which to model her personality, and she had rejected her Aunt. On whom, then, *did* she model herself? My guess is that it was partly her father, and partly Tabby, that outspoken Yorkshirewoman, who were the only two other adults Emily knew.

But in her fantasy world, another influence made its appearance. Emily was greatly attracted imaginatively to the character of the Princess Victoria, heiress to the English throne, whom she saw as a person of round about her own age who would eventually become the most powerful person in the land.

So in Gondal, Princess Victoria formed one of her chief characters, and her land of the imagination was to be governed by a woman, not a man — a woman of great power and strength and influence.

There was no dashing male hero as in Charlotte's fantasy.

In Emily's world, men were not recognised as the dominant sex. Emily knew her own worth, and considered that women could be just as powerful, if not more so, than men. Her own masculine streak persuaded her that she was just as good — if not actually superior — to any man, and she was to persist in this attitude in all her work, throughout her life. She never wanted, or needed, the love of a man.

(ii)

We can deal quite quickly with the events of Emily's life. Apart from Cowan Bridge, she only left the Parsonage on three occasions for any length of time; the rest of her life was spent at home. We have heard that, at the age of seventeen, she accompanied Charlotte to Roe Head — Charlotte, previously a pupil there, was returning as a teacher, and part of her salary was an offer to take one of her sisters as a pupil also. Emily was next in line. However unwilling she was to leave the Parsonage, obviously Emily must go.

Here we see, for the first time outside the Parsonage walls, how different Emily was from other girls of her own age, and, in her way, how much more mature in outlook. She hated school. She had pursued her own lines of thought since she was a child, and found the lessons stupid and irksome, the other girls frivolous and silly, and the idea of living away from the moors impossible.

Even the presence of Charlotte, another member of the Group, did not help her on this occasion, and her longing for Gondal and her "other self" quickly made her ill with homesickness. She stood it for only a few weeks, and within three months, her illness was so great that she was sent home, and Anne took her place.

Later, Charlotte was to describe what she thought was the reason for Emily's illness. We can see that she was near the truth, although of course, she could have had no inkling of her sister's schizoid personality, but she knew something of how much the moors and her home meant to Emily when she wrote:

"My sister Emily loved the moors. Flowers brighter than the rose bloomed in the blackest of the heath for her; out of a sullen hollow in a livid hillside her mind could make an Eden. She found in the bleak solitude many and dear delights; and not the least and best loved — was liberty.

"Liberty was the breath of Emily's nostrils; without it, she perished. The change from her own home to a school, and from her own very noiseless, very secluded, but unrestricted and inartificial mode of life, to one of disciplined routine (though under the kindliest auspices) was what she failed in enduring. Her nature proved here too strong for her fortitude. Every morning when she woke, the vision of home and the moors rushed on her, and darkened and saddened the day that lay before her. Nobody knew what ailed her but me — I knew only too well . . ."

Of course, what Charlotte did not know was that Emily only half existed when deprived of her secondary personality — the moors, home and Gondal — and that she was struggling along with only part of her being while at school. Her identity was cut in half, as it were. But at least Charlotte realized that "I felt in my heart she would die, if she did not go home", and, intuitively understanding her sister's plight, set things right by arranging for Emily's recall to the Parsonage.

★ ★ ★

Once back at home, her personality whole again, Emily was content, and continued to follow her own lines of thought and her own working out of the mystery of the world and the universe in her poetry. Branwell, her brother, was also at home, and she found in him some sort of substitute for the loss of Anne, who had of course, gone to Roe Head in her place.

Branwell proved to be to Emily an interesting study in failure and arrogance, in the collapse of greatness and vanity, for he had just returned from London, where he had confidently been expected by all the family to enroll at the Academy Schools to study art. His nerve had given way, however. He had not even attempted to enroll, but had come home with a trumped-up tale of having been robbed, after spending all the money his father had given him in the Castle Tavern in Holborn.

He was a pitiful creature — deflated, yet still with grandiose dreams, still vain in spite of his moral collapse, and Emily nursed his spirit as she would have nursed a wounded animal or bird from the moors. She watched his reactions to failure, his inability to come to terms with what was expected of him — and yet his supreme confidence that he was still meant for great things.

For, even more than Charlotte, Emily had long ago stepped completely outside of "real life", and as a writer, she too was in a position of a voyeur, who watched others — watched them suffer and try their wings in the world; watched them love and hate; watched their moods, their strivings, their joys and despairs, their successes and failures . . . She listened to Tabby's stories, she stored up cadences of dialect, words and phrases. She had learned, in fact, the technique of a novelist, and was thus able to write with complete conviction about real people when she came to compose her great work WUTHERING HEIGHTS.

★ ★ ★

One might have expected that Emily would have clung even more closely to home after her experience at Roe Head, but in 1837, when she was nineteen, she left the Parsonage once again, this time to take up a position as teacher in Law Hill, a school near Halifax. We may be startled at this, in view of her feelings about the moors, and her schizoid personality, but there were reasons why all the girls in turn took positions as governesses or teachers.

Their father was not rich, and they had known from their early years that they would be expected to earn their own livings. The others sympathized with Emily, but so long as Tabby was capable of looking after the household, they probably felt that she at least aught to make some effort to help to provide for herself — although no-one would have accused her directly of malingering. But they missed their home too, and they had to suffer "exile", and after all, they had all been trained to be teachers.

It is also possible that now that she was getting older, Emily was trying to come to terms with her personality, and trying to force her conscious onto her unconscious will. She may have felt she *aught* to try to free herself from the moors, not realizing what a tremendous effort this would take on her part.

But having a dual, or schizoid personality is not the same thing as having a mental illness. It is similar, perhaps, to being an introvert or an extrovert, and determination on the part of the individual *can* overcome it if the person in question tries hard enough.

And certainly Emily did try — for the reason we have already touched on, perhaps, that the other girls were suffering "in exile", and she felt it her duty to do the same. The choice, however, would have been her own — Aunt's stern moral creed of duty had made no impression on Emily — but she was not a basically selfish person, and if she could earn a little to help the family budget, she probably thought she aught to make the effort, especially as even Branwell had now gone "into exile" too and departed for a position at a boys' school not far from Halifax.

Much of what Emily heard of local history, and experienced at the school was to help her later when she wrote WUTHERING HEIGHTS, but yet again, her own nature proved too strong for her determination. She despised the pupils and the other teachers, and was bitterly homesick. After a period of some six months, she gave in her notice, and returned thankfully home.

★ ★ ★

For the next five years or so, Emily remained at the Parsonage, and a new development occurred in her writing. Since she was thirteen, she had been composing tales about Gondal, and writing poetry on Gondal themes, as well as more personal verse, but unfortunately, all that she and Anne wrote — except for the poems — has been lost or destroyed, so we cannot study their "juvenilia" in the way that we can with the tiny books about Charlotte and Branwell's Angria.

But after Law Hill, Emily began to write of a haunting presence which came to her in visions and glimpses. It has been described variously as mystic, or as of a feeling of communion with Nature which came not from within but from outside herself, or as of a desire for freedom from her earthly body and union with the Infinite.

My interpretation, however, is that it was the dual nature of Emily's personality struggling to become one, and her mind trying to cope, possibly for the first time in her life, with the problem of her identity and her freedom to be herself — a whole person. Such questions as — who am I? What am I? — may have begun to disturb her peace of mind, and once she had glimpsed what it was like to be an independent entity, she yearned for the freedom that she felt when her dual nature merged into one, and the two halves of her being came together.

We can see from her verses that when the fusion of her two selves occurred, it was ecstatic for her, and she spoke of the experience in terms of physical love, but when her secondary self slipped away again, she felt bereft, she felt agonized.

"Oh, dreadful is the check, — intense the agony,
When the ear begins to hear and the eye begins to see;
When the pulse begins to throb, the brain to think again,
The soul to feel the flesh and the flesh to feel the chain!"

What she in fact sought was the unification of her efficient, everyday personality with her emotional nature, which had been, as we have seen, projected into the moors, her pets and nature in general.

For, when free on the moors, as Ellen Nussey commented, she was a different person to the shy, awkward girl who was so afraid of contact with human beings that she never lifted her head when forced to go out shopping, for instance, or exchanged a word with any passers-by; who silently slipped out of a room when strangers were present; who seldom spoke, even to Charlotte's friends, who visited the Parsonage on many occasions, and with whom Emily became familiar.

Emily on the moors was an attractive person who could display a deep sense of humour (probably inherited from Tabby), an enthusiasm and vivacity and child-like glee that amounted to positive gaiety. This was the other side of her dual personality.

Here is Ellen's word-picture of Emily on her first visit to the Parsonage, when Emily was about fifteen:

"Emily had by this time acquired a lithesome graceful figure. She was the tallest person in the house except her father. Her hair, which was naturally as beautiful as Charlotte's, was in the same unbecoming tight curl and frizz, and there was the same want of complexion. She had very beautiful eyes; but she did not often look at you; she was too reserved. Their colour might be said to be dark grey, at other times dark blue, they varied so. She talked very little . . . "

Later, Ellen wrote:

"Her extreme reserve seemed impenetrable, yet she was intensely loveable; she invited confidence in her moral power. Few people have the gift of looking and smiling as she could look and smile. One of her rare expressive looks was something to remember through life, there was such a depth of soul and feeling, and yet such a shyness of revealing herself."

Emily's everyday personality was, as we have previously touched upon, efficient at housework and cooking, mending and sewing, seeing to emergencies, rock-like when others gave way to their emotions, sensible and capable in business affairs. But she never made any attempt to appear feminine or attractive; indeed, she is usually regarded as a masculine sort of person who strode the moors with her dogs, whistling to them to follow her — the sort of lady we would expect to see these days in country tweeds and brogues and a pork-pie hat.

But, this can be laid partly to her having had to model herself on her father and partly on a robust, middle-aged servant. If only her mother, that dainty, fastidious person, had lived and given her the love, the encouragement and appreciation she so sorely needed, Emily Brontë might have grown up to be a beautiful and extremely charming and gracious woman. The foundations were there (we know she had been a pretty child) — but, again as we have heard, the tree was stunted at the root.

From the age of three, her potential as a loving, attractive, feminine person of grace and poise was stifled and shattered by her mother's death. And so, the schizoid "on-looker" who cared nothing about her appearance and could not communicate emotionally with others is what Emily became.

* * *

Her third venture away from home was when she accompanied Charlotte to Brussels in February of 1842, as a pupil at the Pensionnat Heger. She was twenty-three, and she remained in Brussels for nine months, until the death of Aunt Branwell brought both girls home. This time, strangely enough,

Emily did not fall ill on being separated from her beloved moors, but this does not mean that her personality had altered in any dramatic fashion.

Emily did not like Brussels; she did not like M. Heger nor his methods of teaching — and in fact, she made her dislike of him very obvious. Furthermore, she behaved in exactly the same way as usual when confronted with strangers.

For instance, the girls were invited to Sunday dinner each week by Mr and Mrs Jenkins, the British Chaplain and his wife, and were escorted thither by the Jenkins' sons, John and Edward. But Emily would never speak a word to the two young gentlemen, and, as they sat at table, she maintained an absolute silence, contributing nothing, responding to nothing, so it was not very long before the invitations to dinner, which had in fact proved an embarrassment to Charlotte as well, gradually ceased — greatly to the relief of all concerned.

Emily, so Charlotte reported to Ellen, "works like a horse", and this was probably the explanation behind the fact that Emily managed to survive away from home. For the Brussels interlude had a purpose behind it — the girls were preparing themselves for the prospect of setting up their own school at the Parsonage, and with this in mind — the fact that, hopefully, once they were back in England, she would never have to leave home again — Emily must have managed to control her inclination to fall ill when separated from the moors.

I have already explained that a schizoid personality *can* be controlled if there is enough determination behind it, and on this occasion, Emily had a good reason for learning all she could in preparation for a future which would let her remain at the Parsonage for the rest of her life.

She did, however, still need a great deal of moral support from Charlotte, her only link with home, and M. Heger, though recognizing the quality of her mind and the originality of her thoughts, considered that she was very selfish as far as Charlotte was concerned — he, of course, did not understand Emily's particular difficulty in trying to live away from home.

Inevitably, Emily was unpopular. She

refused to give up her study hours in order to teach her music pupils, and insisted on giving them their lessons during their play time. She was ungainly and unattractively dressed, and when they tried to joke with her about her appearance, she simply said: "I wish to be as God made me", and would do nothing to try and change herself. She would not mix with the other pupils, but clung to Charlotte's arm when they walked out to take the air, thus preventing Charlotte from mingling with others who would like to have made friends with her. Emily managed somehow to keep going — but as Charlotte later commented: "She was never happy till she carried her hard-won knowledge back to the remote English village".

And when, in early November, the girls received a letter informing them that their Aunt was seriously ill — followed by another announcing her death — and they made their preparations for returning home, we can be certain that however much Charlotte longed to come back to her "master", Emily was determined that she would never, under any circumstances, return to the Pensionnat Heger, nor to Brussels. Though the school project at the Parsonage failed, Emily did not in fact ever leave home again for more than a day or so during the rest of her life.

We have so far only mentioned the girls' writing as having developed out of their preoccupation with their fantasy worlds, but in fact, writing meant far more to them than simply an outpouring of stories about their imaginary characters. Patrick had been a born writer, and by some mysterious fate or chance, every one of his four surviving children were born writers also.

Writing — first little stories, later poetry and verse, and later still, serious novels intended for publication, was life to the girls, and of the three of them, Charlotte and Emily possessed extraordinary talent, amounting to genius, while even Anne, though not as gifted, was a writer of above average standard for her day.

Branwell wrote prodigiously as a boy, and considered himself a writer of great merit too, but, sadly, he did not possess that vital spark, and in fact, wrote so furiously in his youth that he had written himself out by the time he reached his twenties. Of all the four, Branwell was the only one who had no talent — as can be seen even in his juvenile works and the various poems he attempted. He was also the only member of the Group who never wrote a serious novel. Claims have been made that he wrote at least part of WUTHERING HEIGHTS, but we can dismiss them. WUTHERING HEIGHTS as it stands was Emily's creation, first and last.

★ ★ ★

Emily's reputation as a writer rests upon her poems, and this one book. But what a book! There has never been one like it, and there never will be. It stands alone, and bears no comparison with anything else in English literature.

But it was more than just a novel, although, as a creative writer, Emily was skilled in planning her plot and using various techniques to put across her story.

She made certain that every development — including the legal procedures by which Heathcliff obtained control of the Heights — was absolutely correct; her cast of characters, though a little limited, was varied, and well-rounded; and she knew the author's trick (as did Shakespeare) of emphasizing tragedy by following it with a comic, or lighter scene. Joseph, the servant (a masterpiece of Yorkshire characterization) provided the grim comedy where necessary, and underlined the basic tragedy of the broken romance between Heathcliff and Catherine.

In addition, Emily, who had been an observer all her life, was equally at home in the rough farm kitchen of the Heights and the genteel parlour of Thrushcross Grange. This was one place where Charlotte could not follow her, for Charlotte had never been able to write with conviction about "society", and her "social" characters are not so convincing as her lower classes. But Emily could write with ease about Edgar Linton, and completely understood the gently-nurtured Isabella's fascination with a rogue. All her characters are equally real.

Characters alone, however, do not make a novel, and the quality of WUTHERING HEIGHTS lies in its force, its power, its sweeping moorland setting and — something else; something that makes the book unforgettable, and transforms the reader by giving him an experience he cannot shake off. What is this mysterious "something" that causes WUTHERING HEIGHTS to electrify everyone who peruses its pages?

★ ★ ★

The theme that has made it famous is the love story between Heathcliff and Catherine, but why should one love story be more memorable than any other? Was it the character of Heathcliff, the fallen angel, the rock-like, cruel man whose only tenderness was for Catherine, and who tormented and tortured everyone else, including his own wife, whom he married purely for her money? No — one can, perhaps sympathize with Heathcliff when he loses Cathy, or be fascinated by this study in evil, but one cannot love him.

And yet Catherine *did* love him. — loved him so much that she died of grief at having betrayed him and married Edgar Linton.

"*Why* did you betray your own heart, Cathy?" (Heathcliff cries wildly, as he clings to her on her death-bed). "I have not one word of comfort. You deserve this. You have killed yourself. Yes, you may kiss me and cry; and ring out my kisses and tears: they'll blight you — they'll damn you. You loved me — then what *right* had you to leave me? What right — answer me — for the poor fancy you felt for Linton? Because misery and degradation, and death, and nothing that God or Satan could inflict would have parted us, *you*, of your own will, did it. I have not broken your heart — *you* have broken it; and in breaking it, you have broken mine. So much the worse for me, that I am strong. Do I want to live? What kind of living will it be when you — oh, God! would *you* like to live with your soul in the grave?"

"Let me alone. Let me alone," sobbed Catherine. "If I have done wrong, I'm dying for it. It is enough! You left me too: but I won't upbraid you! I forgive you. Forgive me!"

"It is hard to forgive, and to look at those eyes, and feel those wasted hands," he answered. "Kiss me again; and don't let me see your eyes! I forgive what you have done to me. I love *my* murderer — but *yours*! How can I?"

This is no love as in other love stories. There are no sex scenes in WUTHERING HEIGHTS, no physical union between Cathy and Heathcliff. (In fact, Cathy is carrying Edgar's child when she dies). But we can see from this short extract that the two identify with each other. They belong, as they have belonged all the way through the story — they need no physical union, for they are spiritually united.

In fact, Catherine expresses it even more positively a little earlier in the book, when she tells Ellen Dean, the housekeeper who is the narrator of their story: " . . . he's more myself than I am. Whatever our souls are made of, his and mine are the same; and Linton's is as different as a moonbeam from lightning, or frost from fire."

A few pages later, Catherine continues:

"I cannot express it; but surely you and everybody have a notion that there is or should be an existence of yours beyond you. What were the use of my creation, if I were entirely contained here? My great miseries in this world have been Heathcliff's miseries, and I watched and felt each from the beginning: my great thought in living is himself. If all else perished, and *he* remained, *I* should still continue to be; and if all else remained, and he were annihilated, the universe would turn into a mighty stranger: I should not seem a part of it. My love for Linton is like the foliage in the woods: time will change it, I'm well aware, as winter changes the trees. My love for Heathcliff resembles the eternal rocks beneath: a source of little visible delight, but necessary. Nelly, I *am* Heathcliff! He's always, always in my mind: not as a pleasure, any more than I am always a pleasure to myself, but as my own being . . ."

When Emily was a little girl of three, and her emotional development was arrested, some of her emotions were projected onto the moors and her home, but the remainder of her feelings, which she was unable to give to her lost mother, or later, to a man, remained deep down in her unconscious, unable to escape. When she wrote WUTHERING HEIGHTS, she freed those passions, and it was these, roaring like a mighty torrent through the story, that made each page burn with indelible fire.

People have wondered how a girl who never had a love affair could write of Cathy and Heathcliff as she did, but Emily was, in fact, writing of herself and her schizoid personality (though, of course, unconsciously). She was saying, in effect, "I am two people; we belong together; we must not be separated, or I shall die," and this emotional reality, this flood of desperate yearning that made the two parts of her nature long for unity that would give her her own identity as a single individual, she projected into her two characters — Cathy and Heathcliff. And it was this that gave the story of their love and Heathcliff's revenge on their children its frightening intensity and its tremendous impact.

★ ★ ★

Emily's fury when Charlotte accidentally read some of her private poetry, her adamant refusal (at first) to allow the verses to be published in the little book of poems that the three girls eventually brought out — their first venture into publishing — can be attributed to the fact that she did not want anyone to see her strivings with herself, and her attempts to come to terms with her own identity.

But by the time she came to write WUTHERING HEIGHTS, perhaps she felt she could explain, through the symbolism of her characters, what she was suffering, and how difficult it was for her to live in two worlds at once.

Unfortunately, she did not realize that what she had written was a unique document, something that the public — even the critics — would not be able to penetrate, although her book sold, but because it was regarded as "shocking" rather than on the merits she had intended.

She was to remain misunderstood for many years, and another point she attempted to describe — that a conventional heaven was not where she belonged, nor longed to go, but that heaven to her meant union with her other self — the moors — scandalized her readers. Not one person — not even Charlotte — saw beneath the surface of WUTHERING HEIGHTS, or understood what she was trying to say, and the fact that she had bared her very soul, revealed her inmost thoughts and philosophies and feelings — and had been rejected — naturally had its effect upon her.

She withdrew completely into herself once more, this time in a way that was even more deep than she had been previously, and with a vulnerability that might have made further losses or adverse comments on her work push her over the brink into the serious illness of schizophrenia — if she had lived long enough.

★ ★ ★

But when WUTHERING HEIGHTS was published (along with Anne's AGNES GREY) in December of 1847, Emily's life had only a year left to run, and during the course of that year, she withdrew more and more into herself, and became increasingly odd, taciturn and difficult. She hid behind the pseudonym of Ellis Bell — all the girls had chosen psyeudonyms which might have been masculine or feminine, because of the prejudice of the day against women authors — and when, in July, a dispute arose at the publishing house of Smith, Elder concerning their real identities, Emily resolutely refused to go up to London with Charlotte and Anne to settle it and reveal herself.

The two other girls made the journey by train, and were hailed and feted. But, as Emily always said when urged to go anywhere: "What is the use? Charlotte will bring it home to me." This time, however, when Charlotte was detailing their adventures, and accidentally let slip the fact that she had told the publishers "We are three sisters", and their names, Emily flew into a rage, and would not be appeased by any apology.

She would *not* have her identity revealed to the public. Ellis Bell she was, and Ellis Bell she would remain. She had already been bitterly hurt by the reception of her novel, and even the prospect of having their little volume of poems re-issued under the imprint of Smith, Elder, did not interest her now.

Charlotte wrote to the publishing-house in September that: "The author never alludes to them; or if she does, it is with scorn". No, Emily had laid down her pen after her revelation of her inmost thoughts in WUTHERING HEIGHTS. There has been a suggestion that she was planning a second novel, but this has never been satisfactorily proved, and no trace has ever been found of such a manuscript. Emily was disillusioned, wounded to the soul, and in addition, illness both physical and mental was beginning to insinuate itself relentlessly into her heart and her life.

Then, in September, Branwell, who had become a total wreck due to his drinking and drug-taking; who had survived what he regarded as the loss of the "love of his life" and been unable to fight off the depressions and melancholia that haunted him afterwards; who had degenerated into a ghost of his former swaggering self, and was a menace in the Parsonage, where he kept his father (who insisted on sleeping in the same room) awake most of the night raving and blaspheming, occasionally causing real damage such as when he accidentally set fire to the curtains, and Emily rushed to put it out before their father should see it — for Branwell, after being awake all night, slept most of the day in a drinken stupor: Branwell, fearful and pursued still by the face of dead Maria, terrified at the thought of death, haggard and thin beyond words — Branwell, the brilliant brother who had promised so much and achieved so little — Branwell died on Sunday, 24th September.

Emily appeared to take his death stoically, but Charlotte reacted to the loss of her brother with an attack of what has variously been described as "bilious fever" or "jaundice", which Philip Rhodes comments was "almost certainly a neurotic reaction to stress. It is often a functional disorder based on psychological stress". Philip Rhodes is also of the opinion that Branwell died of tuberculosis, complicated by his drinking and drug-taking, although he was certified as having died of chronic bronchitis and marasmus (wasting of the body).

Was it coincidence that within three months after Branwell's death, Emily too was dead? The Parsonage servants, Martha Brown and her sisters (who were helping out) were of the firm conviction that Emily died of grief for her brother, but Emily was a complex character, and the reasons for her death were obviously not quite as simple as these uncomplicated folk saw it. Yet perhaps Branwell's death did influence Emily to allow herself to begin unconsciously to seek death as the only refuge left to her from her unwanted contact with the outside world and the conflicts of her troubled personality.

She had already explored the subjects of desolation, loneliness and death itself in her poetry and her novel, and held a different view of salvation to that of more pious, conventional people. She had struggled to reconcile the salvation of such a being as Heathcliff, not through his actions when on earth, but because he had lost his elemental harmony of childhood — as indeed had her brother Branwell.

In Branwell's last terrible weeks of moral and physical collapse, Emily was the only member of the family who seemed to understand his anguish and suffering, and to offer him sympathy and support, while the others simply regarded him as beyond help.

But Emily held a much wider view of life — and death — than her sisters; than her father, even, who was a minister. Her own dream of heaven was, as we have mentioned, of peace and calm, of the absolute unity of her dual identity. And after Branwell's death — perhaps coincidentally, perhaps not — she caught a chill on the day of his funeral, which persisted and would not be shaken off, but rapidly turned into a bad cold and cough — the fatal symptoms of the tuberculosis that had already claimed so many other members of her family.

We must bear in mind at this point that Emily had never before been seriously ill — except for her illness when parted from home at Roe Head — and we must consider that a person under stress will, as I have mentioned, often suffer from physical illness. Who knows, exactly, what Emily was thinking and feeling at this time?

Two things had deeply influenced her during the last year — her revelation of her work, which had been completely misunderstood by her readers; and the death of her brother, which had taken place in a horrifying manner. These two, coupled with her own doctrines and philosophies of life, were perhaps enough to make her refuse to try to fight off her illness, and change her horizon from life to death.

She also began to exhibit — if we can deduce correctly from her behaviour — signs that she was drifting mentally into the turmoils of schizophrenia, in the form known as hebephrenia.

I have already explained that a schizoid personality is not an illness in itself, but I must add that a person of this nature would, if they were to become psychotic, develop schizophrenia rather than other mental illnesses such as manic-depressive psychosis or paranoia. All these are serious, and would have made the victim, in the terms of the Brontës' day, be considered "mad" rather than odd, and it is possible that if Emily had continued to live, and had become worse, she would have caused great distress to her family by being regarded as insane.

Hebephronia is characterized by withdrawal, bizarre behaviour and neglect of one's person, and Emily began to display signs of all these in her last few weeks on earth, as well as tuberculosis. She was so withdrawn that she would not speak even when spoken to; she was barely responsive to gifts from Ellen and boxes of books sent from the publishers; she refused all comment on, or treatment for her bodily illness; and she seemed to want to die.

On 2nd November, Charlotte wrote in a letter to her friend Mr Williams at Smith, Elder:

"I would fain hope that Emily is a little better this evening, but it is difficult to ascertain this. She is a real stoic in illness: she neither seeks nor will accept sympathy. To put any questions, to offer any aid, is to annoy; she will not yield a step before pain or sickness till forced; not one of her ordinary avocations will she voluntarily renounce ... When she is ill there seems to be no sunshine in the world for me. The tie of sister is near and dear indeed, and I think a certain harshness of her powerful and peculiar character only makes me cling to her the more ... "

Later, Charlotte was to write:

"The details of her illness are deep-branded in my memory, but to dwell on them, either in thought or narrative, is not in my power. Never in all her life had she lingered over any task that lay before her, and she did not linger now. She sank rapidly. She made haste to leave us. Yet, while physically she perished, mentally she grew stronger than we had yet known her . . . I had seen nothing like it; but indeed, I have never seen her parallel in anything. Stronger than a man, simpler than a child, her nature stood alone. The awful point was that while full of ruth for others, on herself she had no pity; the spirit was inexorable to the flesh . . . ”

★ ★ ★

Yes, Emily wanted to die; she hurried to reach that calm haven where she would be at peace. In spite of her sisters' attempts to make her see a doctor, or obtain medicine for her, she refused everything, and reduced herself to such a state that on Tuesday, 19th December, her body at last gave way. She had refused to stay in bed for one single day of her illness, and was lying on the sofa in the parlour when, about mid-day, she gasped out to Charlotte (probably knowing it was too late): “If you will send for a doctor, I will see him now”.

But before one could be brought, Emily died, at about two o'clock that afternoon, and — we must hope — achieved the harmony and unity of personality she had sought all her life in her own personal heaven.

Part Five

Anne

Anne

(i)

MOST writers who have attempted portraits of the Brontë girls are inclined to dwell at length upon the lives and works of Charlotte and Emily; and to ignore Anne, or simply mention her as an afterthought. She has been portrayed as "gentle", "dove-like", "docile" and other such adjectives which give one the impression that she had little personality, and not very much will of her own when compared to the fiery Charlotte and the monolithic personality of Emily.

Yet Anne, undeniably, was the bravest, the most courageous and the most admirable (from a psychological viewpoint) of all the Brontë sisters. While she faced traumas similar to those suffered by the others, Anne remained in the real world — she did not become neurotic, and she did not try to escape into fantasy.

She simply accepted her lot, and suffered quietly, rarely complaining, yet smarting from wounds that the others were unable to bear, and shouldering her burdens with a resolute determination, while her modest hopes and dreams came to nothing, and she had no shoulder to cry on, nor any assistance from a friend, nor any means of escape from the full reality of her situation.

She was born only a few months before the family moved to Haworth, and in consequence, lost her mother almost before she had come to know her, even as a baby, while her father was his usual aloof self as far as his youngest child was concerned. So Anne's babyhood was spent in the care of Nancy and Sarah, until, when she was about eighteen months old, Aunt Branwell came upon the scene, and Aunt immediately took the frail little creature under her wing.

Anne, a delicate child, became her Aunt's pet, her Aunt's favourite (along with Branwell), her Aunt's little angel.

As far as angels go, there is a story that when Anne was lying in her cradle one day (before the advent of Aunt), Charlotte rushed to tell her father that she had just seen an angel standing alongside her baby sister — but of course, when Patrick investigated, this celestial being had disappeared. However, Anne was to prove that if an angel *had* visited her in babyhood, this shining creature had given her the gifts of virtue and exceptional goodness, and a particularly affectionate nature. She was so frail and undemanding that Charlotte later recalled that "from her childhood, Anne seemed preparing for an early death."

★ ★ ★

Anne might have developed into the happy and contented child her babyhood promised if it had not been for the influence of her Aunt. But Miss Branwell saw in her the incarnation of her sister Maria, the children's mother, and was determined to foster and nurture the little girl into what she regarded as "the ways of goodness" and "the path of duty". The other children had already begun to develop, and were forming their own characters, but Anne was still young enough for her Aunt to shape and mould her mind and heart, and she proceeded to do so.

This would not have mattered if Aunt had been a kindly creature, but unfortunately, as we have already heard, she was a stern and strict Methodist, who had no time for the frivolities of life (except as regarded herself, as one of the "saved") and she preached a doctrine of sin and fear of the wrath of God which the little Anne could barely understand, but which blighted and terrified her. She was so much under her Aunt's influence that she had little chance to hear of a more loving religion.

So in the first five formative years of her life, while the older girls were coping as best they could at Cowan Bridge, and with their psychological difficulties; and while Maria and Elizabeth were dying, the little Anne was struggling with other problems. She was wicked, she was a sinner, she would be damned if she was not good. She must have shed many a tear in private, for life as her Aunt portrayed it seemed awful and gloomy indeed.

Would she ever be saved, or was she to remain one of the damned? These fears were to influence her thinking for the rest of her life, and it is not surprising that she developed both asthma and a stammer. Such illnesses, as we have seen, can often be traced to stress, and the young Anne was definitely under a good deal of stress, spending most of her time, as she did, with her Aunt. Much of her life was to be endured in trembling fear of isolation from God and the dreadful prospect that she — a sinner — would not be able to achieve salvation.

This fear, and the despair that went with it, is to be found in many of her poems; for the years two to seven are those when the child feels itself egocentric, when rules are rules, and the impressions of unworthiness and punishment for naughtiness spread to encompass the whole universe of the child's mind.

Anne did not have to suffer the change of environment to Haworth; nor the sudden departure of a mother she hardly knew, for she was too young and of too contented and adaptable a disposition to brood over psychological problems, as Charlotte and Emily did in their unconscious. Neither did she have to face the trauma of Cowan Bridge, so the result was that she grew up with fewer psychological "hang-ups" — a normal child, in fact — except for the religious fears inculcated by Aunt, and the depressions which, in later life, often accompanied these fears.

We may glimpse her depression and her despair in such lines as:

"Oppressed with sin and woe,
A burdened heart I bear . . . "

and

"I have gone backward in the work,
The labour has not sped;
Drowsy and dark my spirit lies,
Heavy and dull as lead.
"How can I rouse my sinking soul
From such a lethargy?
How can I break these iron chains
And set my spirit free?"

Such lines as these, together with the fact that (for some odd reason) Anne's first novel AGNES GREY is often regarded as rather dull — possibly because of the heroine's austere name; and the fact that a tradition has grown up that Anne's work was very much inferior to that of her brilliant sisters, and she was not very gifted at all artistically, have inclined to suggest that Anne merely trailed at the skirts of Charlotte and Emily, and is hardly worth consideration either as a writer or as a person.

In fact, nothing could be further from the truth. Anne Brontë was the most attractive of the three surviving sisters, both in looks and personality; it is true that she was excessively shy, but the picture that emerges from a study of her character is of a child and a young lady who (when not overshadowed by religious fears, or family tragedy) was loving, open-hearted, brave enough to voice her keenly-felt condemnation of injustice and evil wherever she came across it, and with two attributes which neither Charlotte nor Emily possessed: a courageous, yet not defiant nature which could not be broken by adversity, and a normal young girl's bubbling sense of fun.

To know Anne was to love her, although not many people penetrated behind her reserve and came to know this gentle, yet, steely-hearted young woman who spoke out quietly for what she believed was right, made no fuss, created no scenes — and then, outrageously, was to be condemned by the reading public for writing a "scandalous" and "coarse" book when she published her second novel, THE TENANT OF WILDFELL HALL.

Charlotte herself wrote several appraisals of both Anne's character and her work while her sister was alive, and after she was dead. When Anne, at the age of nineteen, took up her first position as a governess at Blake Hall, Mirfield, Charlotte wrote to Ellen:

"Poor child! She left us last Monday; no-one went with her; it was her own wish that she might be allowed to go alone, as the thought she could manage better and summon more courage if thrown entirely upon her own resources . . . "

Patronizingly, Charlotte added later: "She writes such a clever, sensible letter. It is only the talking." (As we know, Anne, especially when overcome with shyness, had a slight stammer). "I do seriously apprehend that Mrs Ingham will conclude she has a natural impediment of speech."

Of Anne's work, Charlotte was to write in her BIOGRAPHICAL NOTICE OF ELLIS AND ACTON BELL (Acton Bell being Anne's pseudonym) to introduce a new edition of WUTHERING HEIGHTS and AGNES GREY in 1850, when both her sisters were dead:

"THE TENANT OF WILDFELL HALL by Acton Bell, had likewise an unfavourable reception. At this I cannot wonder. The choice of subject was an entire mistake. Nothing less congruous with the writer's nature could be conceived. The motives which dictated this choice were pure, but, I think, slightly morbid. She had, in the course of her life, been called on to contemplate, near at hand and for a long time, the terrible effects of talents misused and faculties abused;" (by this, of course, Charlotte meant Branwell's drunken physical and moral collapse, of which Anne's work was largely a study, intended to show the world the evils of excessive drink) "hers was naturally a sensitive, reserved and dejected nature; what she saw sank deeply into her mind; it did her harm. She brooded over it till she believed it to be a duty to reproduce every detail . . . as a warning to others. She hated her work, but would pursue it. When reasoned with on the subject, she regarded such reasonings as a tempation to self-indulgence. She must be honest; she must not varnish, soften, or conceal."

It is quite obvious, when reading Anne's own revelations about why she had written THE TENANT, and from other references to Anne's work in Charlotte's correspondence, that to Charlotte, Anne was always "the baby" who must be protected from the world (even though she was probably more worldly-wise than Charlotte herself) and that Charlotte never really understood her youngest sister, nor appreciated her writing. She was always patronizing, always convinced that she knew exactly what Anne thought and felt — and usually quite wrong.

Lewis K. Tiffany writes in CHARLOTTE AND ANNE'S LITERARY REPUTATION: "If only she had stuck by her sister and had attempted to defend her work, one wonders how Anne's reputation would have been affected. At the very least Charlotte by so doing would have permitted Anne's work to stand or fall on its own merits . . . But . . . it cannot be denied that Charlotte's harsh critical judgments severely damaged — even down to our own day — Anne's literary reputation." Charlotte was, in fact, Anne's first hostile critic.

★ ★ ★

Not so with Emily, for if we pick up the strands of Anne's life again after the deaths of Maria and Elizabeth, and the return of the older girls from Cowan Bridge, we will find that Emily had not forgotten the little sister who was the one being on earth she had learned to love. Emily was fifteen months older than Anne, and still a child herself, crippled, as we have seen, by her mother's death. But even at this stage in her life, before her dual personality had exerted its clinging grip on the moors, Emily had begun to love nature, and she and Anne together explored the wide, free world which lay outside the door of the Parsonage.

Out there, amid the heather and the rocks and becks and the great expanse of sky, Emily could project the emotion which had no other outlet since her Mama was dead, and Anne could feel that her Aunt's doom-laden vision was perhaps not the complete picture of the prospects of what life held in store for her. Both found great comfort and consolation from natural things — the soaring hawk; the flash of song from the skylark; the soft tinkling of pure water; the little flowers clinging to their precarious crevices amid the harsh heath.

Anne herself used one of her favourite wild flowers as the basis of a romantic incident in AGNES GREY, which was the tale of the trials of a governess's life based on her own experiences, but with a love story interwoven which did not, alas, ever occur in Anne's own governessing days.

" . . . it was a lovely afternoon about the close of March, Mr Green and his sisters had sent their carriage back empty, in order to enjoy the bright sunshine and balmy air in a sociable walk home along with their visitors, Captain Somebody and Lieutenant Somebody else (a couple of military fops), and the Misses Murray, who, of course, contrived to join them. Such a party was highly agreeable to Rosalie;" (Agnes's pupil) "but not finding it equally suitable to my taste, I presently fell back, and began to botanize and entomologize along the green banks and budding hedges, till the company was considerably in advance of me, and I could hear the sweet song of the happy lark; then my spirit of misanthropy began to melt away beneath the soft, pure air and genial sunshine: but sad thoughts of early childhood, and yearnings for departed joys, or for a brighter future lot, arose instead. As my eyes wandered over the steep banks covered with young grass and green-leaved plants, and surmounted by budding hedges,

I longed intensely for some familiar flower that might recall the woody dales or green hill-sides of home: the brown moorlands, of course, were out of the question. Such a discovery would make my eyes gush out with water, no doubt; but that was one of greatest enjoyments now. At length I descried, high up between the twisted roots of an oak, three lovely primroses, peeping so sweetly from their hiding place that the tears already started at the sight; but they grew so high above me, that I tried in vain to gather one or two, to dream over and to carry with me: I could not reach them unless I climbed the bank, which I was deterred from doing by hearing a footstep at that moment behind me, and was, therefore, about to turn away, when I was startled by the words, "Allow me to gather them for you, Miss Grey", spoken in the grave, low tones of a well-known voice. Immediately the flowers were gathered and in my hand. It was Mr Weston, of course — " (the new curate, with whom Agnes is already half in love) " — who else would trouble himself to do so much for *me*?"

Nature, then, helped to soothe away some of the young Anne's fears implanted by her Aunt, and so did the formation of the Group — it comforted her, young as she was, to think that her brother and sisters loved and cherished her, even though she was a sinner. She even began, tentatively, to question some of the precepts her Aunt had laid down as strict and immutable, and for her, the years after Cowan Bridge were, on the whole, happy ones.

She loved the flowers, the scents and sounds around her home, and of course, she and Emily were introduced into the magical world of Glasstown. But it was not until Emily was thirteen, and Charlotte was at Roe Head as a pupil that Emily created the kingdom of Gondal, which was to belong solely to herself and Anne, and was to embody all the things these two — as apart from the Group as a whole — enjoyed, believed and in which they could find their own particular solace against the rest of the world.

(ii)

Unlike Charlotte and Emily, Anne never left home during her growing-up years, and it was not until she was fifteen and was sent to replace the homesick Emily as a pupil at Roe Head that she first ventured into the outside world. Until then, her life had revolved solely around the Parsonage, the village and the moors.

She had been taught by her Aunt, and later by Charlotte when the latter returned from her own period as a pupil at Roe Head; she had become used to the fixed routine of the household; she had, it is true, never known the supportive love of her mother or father, but she had been petted and indulged by Tabby in the warm sanctuary of the kitchen; and she had shared a wide imaginative world with Emily as they walked on the moors and discussed the adventures of the characters of Gondal — around which they now wrote stories and verse, as Charlotte and Branwell had long since been doing

308

about Glasstown and Angria.

Anne's growing-up was a preparation for a future life where she had a deep and sensitive, whole-hearted love to give to the world — she, out of all the girls, might have had a happy married life had fate decreed it.

She did not want revenge and power, as Charlotte did; she did not want to escape, as Emily had done. She was prepared to give her heart into the keeping of some good man whom she could admire and respect — were he rich or poor. Her hero in AGNES GREY, for instance, was a mere curate, not a crippled hawk of a person, full of violence and passion, as was Jane Eyre's Mr Rochester, by the time she married him.

Anne's dreams were modest — a kind husband, a home, perhaps children — but how differently she would have treated her own children from the way in which Aunt had terrified her with visions of sin in her early years!

And it was not as though she was unattractive. When Ellen Nussey made her celebrated first visit to the Parsonage after she and Charlotte had left their schooldays at Roe Head behind them, she found that:

"Anne, dear, gentle Anne, was quite different in appearance from the others. She was her aunt's favourite. Her hair was a very pretty, light brown, and fell on her neck in graceful curls. She had lovely violet-blue eyes, fine pencilled eyebrows, and clear, almost transparent complexion. She still pursued her studies, and especially her sewing, under the surveillance of her aunt." Ellen also commented, as we have heard, that "(Emily) and Anne were like twins — inseperable companions, and in the very closest sympathy, which never had any interruption."

This, then, was the girl who went to Roe Head, where Charlotte was now a teacher, in place of the sick Emily, who could not live without Gondal and the moors. How did Anne fare? She had had a comparatively happy childhood — but alas for poor Anne, *her* trials were largely to come later in her life, not during her early years, as with the others.

★ ★ ★

In her biography ANNE BRONTË, Winifred Gerin has commented on Anne's style of writing, immediately visible to all who have read the Brontë books:

"Anne achieved a distinct style of her own — always fresh and lucid, very often sparkling, and sometimes illuminated by a flash of self-betrayal which, in its naivete, homely wisdom and felicity of phrase, recalls Goldsmith more than any other writer in the English language. Anne Brontë did not hesitate to laugh at herself . . . This, above all, is the point of style which differentiates her from her sisters, and is the true hall-mark of her writing."

We have already mentioned that Anne had a sense of fun, which at times could be sharply satirical, and with her pretty looks, her wide reading (for, like her sisters, she had read a great deal, mainly poetry, and on the forms used by her favourite poets, she had modelled her own verse); her music — for she loved it passionately, and both played and sang a little — drawing-room accomplishments that Charlotte, for instance, never possessed:

311

with all these in her favour, as well as an above average artistic talent, one might have expected Anne to sweep into Roe Head, make friends with everyone, and come away the most popular girl in the school.

But not so. She worked hard, but made no friends and achieved no special praise, nor was singled out for any particular gifts she possessed. She left — when eventually she did leave — as quietly as she had come, having made no special impression on the community.

And yet she had such a lot of love to give! But the reason why she found it so hard to bestow it undoubtedly lay in Anne's extreme shyness and lack of confidence when away from home. She, more than any of the other girls, was her mother's daughter, the child who most resembled dainty, fragile Maria Branwell in her delicate looks and her slender, graceful figure. Anne even possessed her mother's honesty and sincerity of mind, and Aunt had seen to it that she had, too, Maria's extreme religious piety. Even her mother's morbid self-doubt and lack of belief in her own goodness were present in this, her youngest daughter's personality. But whereas Maria had been her own mistress for many years, and had been brought up in a bustling society. Anne's early life had been extremely isolated, and she had been "babied" since childhood because of her poor health, and had not yet managed to achieve the poise and social manners that her mother had possessed when she married Patrick. Anne hid behind a facade of shyness at the age of fifteen — but it was genuine shyness, not affectation.

★ ★ ★

She could express herself well enough in her own writing — indeed, writing gave her an outlet for her feelings and thoughts — and she did not under-value herself as a person. In fact, she and Emily had come to various conclusions about the position of women in society during their creation of Gondal and its development, which, when later incorporated into their work (especially Anne's TENANT) were to scandalize the general public. In feminist thinking, they were innocently far ahead of their time. But to hold her own in a real-life conversation or situation was something Anne was unable to do easily, if at all.

She herself confessed to Ellen in a letter: " . . . you must know there is a lamentable deficiency in my organ of language which makes me almost as bad a hand at writing as talking unless I have something particular to say."

Charlotte explained Anne's shyness in this way: "A constitutional reserve and taciturnity placed and kept her in the shade, and covered her mind, and especially her feelings, with a sort of nun-like veil which was rarely lifted."

And finally, we have the opinion of a man of the world, none other than Charlotte's publisher, the dashing George Smith, who met Anne on one occasion — when she and Charlotte paid that momentous first visit to London (there were to be many others for Charlotte, but none for Anne) to prove that the Bells were "three sisters" and not all one person. We have already heard that Mr Smith — with some perspicacity — was later to deduce that Charlotte would have given all her fame and genius to have been beautiful. He wrote of Anne:

"She was a gentle, quiet, rather subdued person, by no means pretty but of a pleasing appearance . . . Her manner was curiously expressive of a wish for protection and encouragement, a kind of constant appeal, which invited sympathy."

So we must try to look on Anne as a person whose "iron hand" — if we can thus describe her strong feelings, her many talents, her keen, logical mind, her powers of observation and her ability as a writer — were forever hidden (except in the company of Emily) beneath a "velvet glove" of shyness, which gave the impression of insipidness and lack of personality with which Anne has often been regarded.

We can imagine what reserves of courage it took a girl of this nature to go out alone into the world and face strangers — both when she went to Roe Head, and later in her various positions as governesses!

Anne was just as unhappy at school as Emily had been, but she plodded on silently, making no complaint. Charlotte, whose presence should have been a help to her, was deeply involved in her own emotional problems of frustration as a writer, as well as psychological difficulties, and she did not have time to notice that Anne was, perhaps, quieter and more withdrawn than usual. In fact, Anne was going through a dark and melancholy period of religious doubts.

She had come to sense the presence of a kind and benevolent God through Nature, but, deprived of Emily's company and the moors, all her Aunt's gloomy teachings of her early years came flooding into her brain, and she suffered agonies of forboding and fear lest she should be too much of a sinner to gain salvation. She wrote many verses on the subject of her fears and depression, but confided in no-one, and the result was that eventually, she became ill as her unconscious mind tried to cope with her mental turmoil.

She asked to see a minister, and

the Reverend James La Trobe, the Moravian bishop who came to her, reported later that: "She was suffering from a severe attack of gastric fever which brought her very low, and her voice was only a whisper; her life hung on a slender thread." Fortunately, the Moravian theology was one of love and hope, and "her heart opened to the sweet views of salvation, pardon and peace in the blood of Christ, and she accepted His welcome to the weary and heavily laden sinner, conscious more of her not loving the Lord her God than of acts of enmity to Him, and, had she died then, I should have counted her His redeemed and ransomed child."

Anne clung to this gospel of love, which her heart told her was true, and, thanks to the visits of the Rev. La Trobe, she was able to free herself a great deal from the dark toils of Aunt's religious terrors. From then on, her religion became one of the great consolations of her life, though from time to time, Aunt's teachings, implanted in childhood, were to raise their heads and cause her doubt and suffering.

But, resolutely, Anne clung to hope,

and fought them off, and by the time of her death, she was able to accept the promise of salvation, and to face her departure from this world with the conviction that her sins were forgiven and she would not be utterly damned. It is good to know that eventually, she died quietly, and at peace.

★ ★ ★

She recovered from her illness, but later, while still at school, became ill again, suffering from a cold, cough, and difficulty in breathing. Once more, she made no complaint, but Charlotte could not help but notice her sister's plight, and with the memory of the deaths of Maria and Elizabeth in her mind, she instituted the famous scene with Miss Wooler, where she accused the headmistress of not caring about Anne's illness — among other things. The result was that both girls returned to the Parsonage.

Charlotte, as we have heard, went back to the school and tried to carry on teaching, until she fell ill herself, and had to leave the school for good in order to save her sanity, her life, or both.

Meanwhile, Anne relaxed in the peace and seclusion of the Parsonage, and remained at home for two years, regaining her health and strength — continuing, of course, with writing her poetry and stories of the Gondal saga. She had her new belief in the love of God to sustain her, she had the moorlands to wander, and the joys of nature to appreciate, as well as the company of Emily for part of the time, when Emily was not away teaching at Law Hill. Life was busy and happy.

But Anne was very conscious that she must do as the others were doing, and try to earn her own living, and on reaching the age of nineteen, she announced her intention of looking for a post as a governess — much to the consternation of the rest of the family, who had always regarded her as particularly frail, and did not want to see her going "into exile". After all, she had suffered two serious illnesses while at school. Would she be able to manage alone, away from home, cut off from the rest of them?

But Anne, in her quiet way, was determined. She would not be a burden. She had been trained to earn her living, and she felt that the time had come to put her training to some use. Charlotte was looking for another post — so she would do the same.

And so, on 8 April, 1839, Anne left for Blake Hall, Mirfield, where she was to have the charge of the two elder children in the Ingham family which resided there — a boy aged six, and a girl aged five. She was prepared to love her charges, for as we know, she had a lot of love to give — but she found this impossible. The children were unruly little demons who made her life a misery, and just before Christmas of that year, much to her chagrin — but also to her deep relief, she was dismissed, and returned home bloody, but unbowed, consoling herself with the thought that "surely all children could not be like that!"

The exploits of the young Inghams to hurt, humiliate and upset her were detailed in AGNES GREY in the characters of the little Bloomfields, and some people declared that these characters were so bullying, sadistic and bad that they could not possibly be based on real children. But Anne herself admitted that they were, and a descendant of the family, Susan Brooke, has written a confirmation that the way of life as described by Anne at Blake Hall was acutely observed and absolutely true. Susan Brooke adds:

"When thinking of the old days in the house which no longer exists, one cannot help feeling that Anne Brontë was one of the few people who saw that all was not well with the children's upbringing. She had the courage to warn the parents without fearing for her own position, whereas many governesses would have taken the easier way described by Charlotte of saying nothing and making themselves as comfortable as possible. Far from being over-imaginative, she had the perception and foresight that might have helped to avert more than one tragedy, and could have prepared a happier pattern for the future. The main things she lacked were encouragement, support and experience. These were denied her by the nature of the environment, mainly because she refused to compromise with what she considered cruelty and injustice."

★ ★ ★

After her dismissal from Blake Hall, Anne was glad to return home to the security of the Parsonage, but less than two years later, she again attempted the life of a governess, this time at Thorp Green Hall, with a family called Robinson, who had four children, all older than her previous pupils, and here again, she called upon her experiences when describing Agnes's second situation as a governess at a house she called "Horton Lodge", which possessed fictitious inhabitants named Murray.

Once more, she was prepared to love her pupils, but, as before, her situation was uncongenial to her, her charges shallow and headstrong, but she managed to persevere for four years, (except for holidays at home) although often she felt depressed and discouraged. She even managed to obtain a post for Branwell as tutor to the Robinsons' little boy, Edmund — which, though she did not know it, was to lead to tragedy. Later, Anne was to write: "During my stay . . . I have had some very unpleasant and undreamt-of experiences of human nature . . ."

For Branwell fell madly in love — or thought he was in love — with Mrs Robinson, and we can be certain that Anne knew at least something of the goings-on between her brother and her employer's wife, who was nearly twenty years his senior. The situation became intolerable to her, and in the summer of 1845, she gave in her notice. Branwell accompanied her home, but returned alone to his "adored Lydia", leaving Anne deeply disturbed and with a terrible sense that she had failed to save him from a course of action that could only lead to disaster — as indeed, it did, for Branwell was dismissed in disgrace, and from then on, his descent into brooding and melancholy at being parted from his "lost love" led him into a frenzied pattern of drinking and drug-taking which was to help bring about his death.

★ ★ ★

The dismal four years as a governess had given Anne much, however. She had become familiar with the way of life in a large household, and the behaviour of "society people", so that later, she was to be able to create convincingly the characters and life-style of such people in THE TENANT OF WILDFELL HALL.

She had also made the discovery that the sea was to be a revelation and an inspiration to her when she visited fashionable Scarborough with her charges, and saw the ocean for the first time. She used the sea-shore as a setting for the final scene in AGNES GREY; and it was to Scarborough that she expressed a desire to go when, four years later, she knew she was dying. She is the only member of the Brontë family whose grave is not in Haworth.

★ ★ ★

On Aunt's death, she had left each of the girls a little money, and there was no need now for Anne to go "into exile" again. Already she had started to write what was to become AGNES GREY, and for the remainder of her short life, she was busy with her career as a writer.

AGNES GREY was published in 1847, and Anne immediately began work on THE TENANT. Her subject was constantly before her eyes, for Branwell had become a menace to the whole family, and Anne felt it her duty to try and warn the world of the evils of dissipation and drink as she watched her wretched brother day by day.

It was not a happy time, but Anne felt she had undertaken a worthwhile task, and was satisfied with her work when THE TENANT was published in 1848. No doubt thoughts of a new book were in her mind, but towards the end of that year, Branwell died, Emily died, and Anne recognized in herself the dreaded symptoms of tuberculosis. In May of 1849, she was dead.

In the period between her two posts "in exile", Anne was, of course, at home in the Parsonage, and on her arrival back from Blake Hall at Christmas in 1839, she first met the young man who had become her father's curate the previous August. His name was Willy Weightman, and he was in his mid-twenties, merry and flirtations, but with excellent references as a scholar. His presence at the Parsonage was to prove a breath of fresh air that blew away all cobwebs of brooding and melancholy, and gave new life to the girls as rain to thirsty flowers. Everyone liked him — and it is generally believed that Anne very quickly fell in love with him.

We have already mentioned that Anne had a great store of love to give, but so far in her life (she was then just twenty years old) she had been unable to bestow it upon anyone except Emily, and to a slightly lesser degree, Charlotte, Branwell and Tabby. But loving her family was, of course, quite different to loving a man with the possibility of becoming his wife, and there is no mention anywhere that Anne had ever before felt attracted to a male in this particular way.

If we look a little closer, this may seem rather odd. Anne had, it is true, spent only a short period away from home, but she must have met visitors to the Parsonage, and other young men during her time at Blake Hall. And the teen years are when romantic and sexual feelings stir in a young girl. Even Charlotte had her erotic fantasies about the magnificent Zamorna. But Gondal, the kingdom of Emily and Anne, appears to have been curiously sexless, and Anne seems to have had no fantasies or romantic attachments before, however slight, to any young man she had ever met.

And then, so popular belief says, she fell madly in love with Willy Weightman almost as soon as she set eyes on him. But there was a snag, for Mr Weightman appears to have had an "understanding", if he was not actually betrothed, to a young lady named Agnes Walton, whom he had left behind in his native Westmorland.

Not that this bothered *him*, however,

for during his time in Haworth, he had already begun flirtations with several other young ladies in the area, and established free-and-easy friendships with the Brontë girls, who called him "Miss Celia Amelia".

★ ★ ★

The atmosphere during the following year, enlivened by Mr Weightman's presence, was one of lightness and fun. He sent the girls valentines (the first they had ever had in their lives); he declared himself "smitten" by Ellen Nussey when she paid a visit to the Parsonage in the spring; he joked and laughed and christened Emily "the Major" when she decided it was her duty to chaperone Mr Weightman and Ellen during their walks on the moor, which were now lively excursions. He made arrangements for a little more social life for them.

Once back at the Parsonage, Anne was naturally included in the activities and revels, but it must have been obvious to her that — whether she loved him or not — Mr Weightman certainly did not pine for *her*. If she had wished to flirt, he would have flirted as cheerfully with her as he did with any other young lady who was prepared to enter into this agreeable pastime, but Anne did not flirt. If she had any feelings for him, she kept them strictly to herself, and even wrote a poem called SELF-CONGRATULATION, in which she admired her own capability in showing no emotion whatsoever when in the presence of this man she, supposedly, loved. She said nothing; she told no-one; she kept her own council, and the result was that to Mr Weightman, she was just shy little Miss Anne, one of "the girls", his superior's daughters — no-one, in fact, had any idea at all what she was thinking or feeling.

"They little knew my hidden thoughts;" she wrote.
"And they will *never* know
"The aching anguish of my heart,
"The bitter burning woe!"

We are here set with an interesting problem. Tradition will have it that it was Willy Weightman whom Anne loved, and in the absence of other contenders, there is no reason to suppose tradition to be wrong; it appears that she was certainly eating her heart out for some young man, this much we know on the slender evidence she left to us. But why, out of all the men she might have chosen to fall in love with, did she chose one who was out of her reach? It is no answer to say that one cannot help falling in love; there is usually some reason, unconscious though it may be, why people are attracted to each other. And one is tempted to the conclusion that Anne deliberately (though quite unconsciously) allowed herself to love the one man whom she knew she could never possess.

This may have sprung from her childhood at home, when she, as well as the other little Brontës, grew up with feelings of insecurity and inferiority; it may have been that Aunt's teachings twisted themselves into some sort of conviction in her unconscious that it was not her fate in life to ever achieve what she desired: but the most likely reason is because, although she was never to try and escape from the world like Emily, she put herself into a situation where, by directing her feelings towards a person she could never have, she could allow herself the luxury of loving, but was safe in the knowledge that she would never have to deal with the realities of her emotions — something, perhaps, which would have been beyond her psychological capabilities.

★ ★ ★

We have portrayed Anne as the most "normal" of the four Brontë children, but she was still a Brontë, a member of the Group; she still suffered from deprivation of her parents' love and an extremely isolated childhood. Even she was to prove unable to face normal interpersonal relationships — especially in the case of loving a man. That she probably did love Willy Weightman, and loved him with a deep and lasting devotion, we can take as almost certain. But many deprived people search for what they feel life has denied them — and discover, if eventually they find it, that there are related things, feelings and emotions, with which they are quite unable to cope.

This was the case with Anne. If Mr Weightman had gone down on his knees and formally declared his love for her (something she knew with unconscious relief would never happen), it is interesting to speculate how she would have responded. She would not have believed him; she would have been convinced he was joking; she would have panicked, told him to go away, refused to listen. What we can be reasonably certain she would *not* have done was to fall into his arms, allow herself to admit she loved him too, and lived happily married to him ever after!

It is claimed that her character of Mr Weston in AGNES GREY was a portrait of Willy Weightman, but if we examine it, we will see that Anne has dwelt on Mr Weightman's more serious, compassionate side (for he did possess those qualities and made an admirable curate) rather than his spirited, frivolous nature. He is represented as reserved, quiet, dignified. Anne as a writer felt that this way she could control him as she would never have been able to control his human ebullience in real life, and in her unconscious mind, she preferred to endure the very painful pangs of unrequited love, and allow herself the luxury of writing poetry to her loved one, suffering silently — rather than abandon her love as hopeless, or think that perhaps there might one day be another man.

The only picture we have of the two together is in a letter from Charlotte to Ellen, where Mr Weightman is making eyes at Anne — perhaps because she was always so reserved when in his company that he just could not resist trying to gain her admiration (little knowing she was pining of love for him).

"He sits opposite Anne at Church sighing softly and looking out of the corners of his eyes to attract her attention; and Anne is so quiet, her look so downcast, they are a picture."

But even Charlotte never dreamed that there was more to this little scene than appeared on the surface, and Anne departed for her second position as a governess without anyone — least of all

Mr Weightman himself — having guessed her secret.

★ ★ ★

There is something about possessing an unrequited love that is almost as good as the real thing — much better for a person who cannot face the realities of interpersonal emotions; and the following year, Anne's secret passion received the final seal which would make it a lifelong thing of bitter-sweetness for her, when the young curate she remembered so wistfully died of cholera at Haworth, sincerely mourned by both Mr Brontë and Branwell. Anne received the news at Thorp Green Hall, probably in a letter, and her own grief must have been sharp and deep, but she kept her sorrow to herself, as she kept everything, and told no-one. Parted from her family, she had no confidante, no-one to whom she could open her heart, only her own reserves of courage to draw on — that and her writing. But the pain she felt was too raw, the wound too sore, for her to think of writing of him yet.

Later, however, she penned various tributes to the man whose memory she was to love faithfully all the rest of her short life.

"Yes, thou art gone! and never more
"Thy sunny smile shall gladden me;
"But I may pass the old church door,
"And pace the floor that covers thee,

"May stand upon the cold, damp stone,
"And think that, frozen, lies below
"The lightest heart that I have known,
"The kindest I shall ever know . . . "

When a loved one, particularly a husband or lover, dies, a strange thing happens once the first shock is over, and Anne would have found this in the case of Willy Weightman, even though she had never admitted her affection to him. All the human faults and failings fall away, for the departed will not now argue or disagree or do anything to spoil the picture the surviving partner chooses to retain in his or her mind. A dead love can be stored, as it were, behind glass, it will never change but will remain comfortingly and reassuringly static in a world of uncertainty. Moreover, the loved one, having left this world, can never go away within it, so the survivor will never be deprived of the object of his or her devotion. This can spell security even if, as in Anne's case, the love was not mutual but one-sided; and even if she had lived to be ninety, she would certainly have clung to her adored Mr Weightman and never wanted to look at another man, for her memory would have provided her with a talisman that made her feel she did not have to seek love any more, she had loved once, and could carry the departed young curate with her (albeit sorrowing over his death, which in itself would have given her a satisfactory conviction that as she had loved him, she had the priviledge to miss him more than anyone else), for ever in her heart. It would probably have been a relief to her unconsciously that she did not have to face the possibility of reality intruding and having to be dealt with in any further male-female relationships. She had had one: she need not prove anything to herself by seeking any more.

Second-best her dead, undeclared love might seem, but it was all that poor Anne could cope with. So Anne's "love affair" suffered the same fate as Charlotte's — though more silently — and Anne too was to expiate her feelings (real or exaggerated) in her novel AGNES GREY. Mr Weston was not Willy Weightman — but he was Willy Weightman as Anne saw him with the eyes of love and the eyes of a writer; and she gave Agnes's story the happy ending which fate and her own nature had denied to her.

★ ★ ★

It has been said that an artist must suffer in order to write great literature; and these three frail girls all produced works that in their way, bore the hall-mark of genius. Anne's were, perhaps, dainty little water-colours in pastel shades — though THE TENANT can be claimed to be a great book.

Emily's WUTHERING HEIGHTS resembles a gigantic sculpture torn from the rock, to stand, elemental and eternal; while Charlotte's works have the polish and finish of paintings in oils, by a master hand . . .

But one thing is certain. They all suffered. And none of them ever found in this world the love for which they had longed since they were born.

Conclusion

IT will be obvious from this book that the parental figures in the lives of the Brontë girls failed utterly to give them the love which would have made them normal, happy people, and that Patrick was never loved by them as a father.

He provided the domineering patriarchal head of the house to which they looked up with respect; he commanded their obedience and their duty; he tyrannized them so that they were never able to enter into satisfactory personal relationships with other men. The girls, especially Charlotte, who lived longest, remained under his influence and never left him even on her marriage — instead, she and her husband settled in at the Parsonage to try and ease the old man's declining years. Patrick had long since become a tyrant.

He had, it is true, suffered much in his long life. His career — particularly as a writer — had come to nothing.

339

His beloved son had died in distressing circumstances, having failed in all his undertakings. Did Patrick ever read WUTHERING HEIGHTS or Anne's two books? We do not know — but all three had been largely condemned by the critics as "scandalous" and "evil".

Patrick lived between 1848 and the rest of his life vicariously through the fame of his successful daughter, Charlotte, who had achieved what he had never been able to do, and conquered the literary world. When she, too, died, he perpetuated her memory by commissioning one of her friends, another well-known and respected authoress, to write the story of her life. (It is significant that he did not ask her to write the lives of all three of his daughters. No, the book was to be Charlotte's alone). The result, Mrs Gaskell's "LIFE OF CHARLOTTE BRONTË, was to become one of the masterpieces of English literature.

★ ★ ★

Their father valued the drawings and paintings and possessions of his dead children, and undoubtedly mourned his daughters — yet he had never known them, only as docile and obedient handmaidens to his whims and will. Mary Taylor, Charlotte's life-long friend, wrote to Ellen: "I can never think without gloomy anger of Charlotte's sacrifices to the selfish old man", and it is true that in the Parsonage, duty to Papa came first with all the girls.

But, strangely, it was this very lack of love from their parents (poor Maria, of course, being dead); this intellectual preoccupation he took in them as children; this almost clinical insistence on the mind rather than the body, that gave the children their first inclinations to write. By allowing them to read freely, and leaving them alone most of the time, he created the opportunity and means for the Glasstown chronicles and later the Gondal saga — and later still, their novels — to emerge.

So we can say with certainty that if they had not had Patrick and Maria as their parents; if Maria had not died; if they had not been subjected to such parental deprivation and isolation in their childhood, the possibility is that some of the greatest English novels would never have been written. The children might well have lived happier lives, but we would have no WUTHERING HEIGHTS, no JANE EYRE, no TENANT OF WILDFELL HALL.

But who is to say whether our loss would have been worth their gain? Who, in fact, is to say that we do not owe Patrick Brontë an immense debt that literature can never repay?

He may have witheld love from his daughters — but he gave them, unknowingly, the gift of immortality.

Bibliography of Works Consulted

Works by the Brontës

THE BRONTË SISTERS: selected poems of Charlotte, Emily and Anne Brontë, edited by Stevie Davies (Fyfield Books/ Carcanet Press 1976)

A selection of the JUVENILIA by Charlotte and Branwell Brontë at Haworth Parsonage Museum Library.

A selection of the poems, sermons and prose writings of PATRICK BRONTË.

THE ADVANTAGES OF POVERTY IN RELI-GIOUS CONCERNS by Maria Branwell.

WUTHERING HEIGHTS (with Selected Poems) by Emily Brontë (Dent: London — Everyman's Library 1971)

JANE EYRE by Charlotte Brontë (Penguin Books)

THE PROFESSOR and EMMA: A Fragment, by Charlotte Brontë (Dent: London — Everyman's Library 1969)

SHIRLEY by Charlotte Brontë (Oxford University Press)

VILLETTE by Charlotte Brontë (Dent: London — Everyman's Library 1969)

AGNES GREY by Anne Brontë (Oxford University Press 1974)

THE TENANT OF WILDFELL HALL by Anne Brontë (The Zodiac Press 1974)

Other works consulted during the writing of this book

STRIVING TOWARDS WHOLENESS by Barbara Hannah (George Allen & Unwin Ltd — 1972)

THE BRONTË STORY by Margaret Lane (William Heinemann 1953)

THE BRONTËS by Brian Wilks (Hamlyn 1975)

I'M OK — YOU'RE OK by Thomas A. Harris (Jonathan Cape 1967)

THE BRONTËS by Phyllis Bentley (Pan Books — 1973)

A MAN OF SORROW by John Lock and W. T. Dixon (Nelson 1965)

THE ART OF WRITING MADE SIMPLE by Geoffrey Ashe (W. H. Allen 1972)

UNQUIET SOUL by Margot Peters (Hodder & Stoughton Ltd 1975)

THE LIFE OF CHARLOTTE BRONTË by Mrs Gaskell (Dent)

EMILY BRONTË: A Psychological Portrait, by Norma Crandall (Richard R. Smith Publisher, Inc.)

THE INFERNAL WORLD OF BRANWELL BRONTË by Daphne du Maurier (Victor Gollancz 1960)

YOUR GROWING CHILD AND RELIGION by R. S. Lee (Macmillan, USA, 1963)

CHILDREN UNDER STRESS by Sula Wolff (Penguin Books 1969)

THE ORIGINS OF LOVE AND HATE by Ian D. Suttie (Kegan Paul 1935)

SOCIAL DEVELOPMENT IN YOUNG CHILDREN by Susan Isaacs (London, Routledge, 1933)

HUMAN SOCIETY by Kingsley Davis (New York, Macmillan 1948)

HUMAN GROUPS by W. J. H. Sprott (Penguin Books 1958)

CHARLOTTE BRONTË by Margaret Howard Blom (Twayne Publishers)

THE BRONTËS' WEB OF CHILDHOOD by Fannie E. Ratchford (Columbia University Press 1941)

CHARLOTTE BRONTË'S WORLD OF DEATH by Robert Keefe (University of Texas Press)

THE HEALTH AND FITNESS HANDBOOK edited by Miriam Polunin (Frances Lincoln/Windward)

EMILY BRONTË by Winifred Gerin (Clarendon Press, Oxford 1971)

ANNE BRONTË by Winifred Gerin (Thomas Nelson and Sons Ltd 1959)

EMILY AND ANNE BRONTË by W. H. Stevenson (Routledge & Kegan Paul)

BRIEF LIVES OF THE BRONTËS by Royston Millmore (Privately printed)

THE INNER WORLD OF CHILDHOOD by Frances G. Wickes (D. Appleton — Century Company Inc. 1937)

THE EXPERIENCE OF REALITY IN CHILDHOOD SCHIZOPHRENIA by Austin M. des Lauriers (Tavistock Publications 1959)

THE BRONTËS by Tom Winnifrith (Collier Books 1977)

THE BRONTËS AND THEIR BACKGROUND by Tom Winnifrith (Macmillan 1977)

EMILY by Dilys Gater (Robert Hale)

The books are listed in the order in which they are mentioned in the text. Any not specifically mentioned in the text come at the end.

The Brontë Society Transactions

The following papers were found to be of particular interest:

THE WEARY ARE AT REST by Thomas Olsen (Vol 10. Part 55)

THE MATERNAL RELATIVES OF THE BRONTËS by J. Hambley Rowe (Vol 6. Part 33)

THE RELATIVES OF MARIA BRANWELL by C. W. Hatfield (Vol 9. Part 49)

A MEDICAL APPRAISAL OF THE BRONTËS by Philip Rhodes (Vol 16. Part 2)

TABITHA AYKROYD by C. Mabel Edgerley (Vol 10. Part 51)

CHARLOTTE AND ANNE'S LITERARY REPUTATION by Lewis K. Tiffany (Vol 16. Part 84)

ANNE BRONTË AT BLAKE HALL — AN EPISODE OF COURAGE AND INSIGHT by Susan Brooke (Vol 13. Part 68)

Acknowledgements

I should like to place on record my thanks to the staff at the Brontë Parsonage Museum for their kindness and invaluable assistance during my visits to Haworth. I also owe an immense debt to the many books I have studied and especially those from which I have quoted, and I thank their authors and publishers most sincerely. Many other people contributed at various times towards the progress of this book, and my thanks goes to them all.

Books by Dilys Gater
Published by The House of Ulverscroft:

PREJUDICED WITNESS
THE DEVIL'S OWN
SOPHY
A BOOK CASE: A POPULAR AUTHOR'S
SUCCESS STORY
THE DARK STAR
THE LURE OF THE FALCON
THE EMILY EXPERIMENT
A PLACE OF SAFETY
THE WITCH-GIRL

Under the Name of Dilys Gater
& Terry Roche:

THE YEAR'S AT THE SPRING

Under the Name of Dilys Gater
& Richard Lawler:

ZODIAC

Other titles in the
Ulverscroft Large Print Series:

TO FIGHT THE WILD
Rod Ansell and Rachel Percy

Lost in uncharted Australian bush, Rod Ansell survived by hunting and trapping wild animals, improvising shelter and using all the bushman's skills he knew.

COROMANDEL
Pat Barr

India in the 1830s is a hot, uncomfortable place, where the East India Company still rules. Amelia and her new husband find themselves caught up in the animosities which seethe between the old order and the new.

THE SMALL PARTY
Lillian Beckwith

A frightening journey to safety begins for Ruth and her small party as their island is caught up in the dangers of armed insurrection.